AF574616

MACON

Celebrates the Millennium

The Greater Macon Chamber of Commerce and Community Communications, Inc., would like to express our gratitude to these companies for their leadership in the development of this book.

COLISEUM HEALTH SYSTEM

Coliseum Medical Centers • Macon Northside Hospital • Middle Georgia Hospital

Sponsored by the Greater Macon Chamber of Commerce.
Photo by Woody Marshall

A special thanks to Bank of America for its support as a patron of Macon Celebrates the Millennium.

Photo by Ken Krakow

MACON

Celebrates the Millennium

By Tracy Maurer
Corporate profiles by Barbara Thompson
Featuring the photography of Ken Krakow

Community Communications, Inc.
Publisher: Ronald P. Beers

Staff for *Macon Celebrates the Millennium*

Acquisitions	Henry S. Beers
Publisher's Sales Associates	John Hecker, Mel Merk, and Richard Tarantino
Editor in Chief	Wendi L. Lewis
Managing Editor	Amy Newell
Profile Editor	Amanda J. Burbank
Design Director	Scott Phillips
Designer	Eddie Lavoie
Photo Editors	Eddie Lavoie and Amy Newell
Contract Manager	Christi Stevens
National Sales Manager	Bob Sadoski
Sales Assistant	Sandra Akers
Acquisitions Assistant	Angela P. White
Proofreaders	Heather Ann Edwards and Carolyn Phillips
Editorial Assistants	Krewe Maynard and Eleanor Parker
Accounting Services	Stephanie Perez
Print Production Manager	Jarrod Stiff
Pre-Press and Separations	DCR Graphics, Inc.

Community Communications, Inc.
Montgomery, Alabama

David M. Williamson, Chief Executive Officer
Ronald P. Beers, President
W. David Brown, Chief Operating Officer

Published 2001
Printed in USA
First Edition
Library of Congress Catalog Number: 2001000296
ISBN: 1-58192-034-2

Photo by Ken Krakow

TABLE OF CONTENTS

• Photo by Ken Krakow

PART ONE

• Photo by Ken Krakow

WILLIAM M. WADLEY

FOREWORD

As residents of Macon enter the new millennium, we are fortunate to be in such a good place at such a good time. We have seen major changes in the economy, and we have seen Macon change in size and attitude—from a small town to a thriving business center of the South. Located near Georgia's midpoint on the Fall Line, Macon historically has occupied a position of prominence in Georgia's geography and its business leadership. The Chamber is poised to lead the city as it moves forward.

The mission of the Chamber is to advance the economic, civic, and cultural growth of central Georgia, to enhance the quality of life in the community, and to foster continuous improvement of the greater Macon area as a place in which to live and conduct business. Many community partners, including the Macon Economic Development Commission, support the Chamber in this mission. To achieve its goals, the Chamber also is committed to support business-to-business relationships, to enhance our position to state developers and prospects, and to be the economic development driver in central Georgia. We want everyone to know that Macon is the ideal place to do business and to raise a family, and that the quality of life here is second to none.

We believe that as you read through this book, you will see this all is true. As these pages show you, Macon has the environment and infrastructure to foster the growth of businesses in a number of ways. We have several major initiatives under way. In addition to the efforts of the Downtown Council and the Urban Development Authority, NewTown Macon is providing the structure for downtown redevelopment. The Ocmulgee Greenway and the River Walk will provide new life along the river, and the Tubman African American Museum will break ground for a multimillion-dollar facility.

The Macon-Bibb County Convention and Visitors Bureau, through its ambassador Richard Little and its "Song and Soul of the South" campaign, is bringing more and more tourists to Macon. In Macon, we have many avenues to explore culture through our rich history and historic homes, museums, the arts, theater, and music. Excellent places to dine and shop and seasonal festivals offer even more entertainment.

The Greater Macon Chamber of Commerce invites you to view our book and come visit us. We hope you enjoy our lifestyle, and we welcome you to stay a while.

Photo by Ken Krakow

PREFACE

When my husband and I first moved to Macon, a tour guide told us that early Native Americans believed drinking the water here connected a person to this place forever. I never found any written record of the prophecy, but I know it holds some truth.

Macon makes an indelible impression in many different ways. This book attempts to highlight the city's fascinating facts, stories, and achievements in a limited space. Any oversight or misinterpretation was unintentional, certainly. Perhaps this brief introduction to the city's charms will whet the appetite for more—and a drink of water as well.

— Tracy Maurer

Photo by Ken Krakow

N67006

CHARTER MEDICAL

PART ONE

Photo by Ken Krakow

CHAPTER ONE

1

A History of Hospitality

Macon presides graciously over the Fall Line, a convergence of geological formations along Georgia's midsection tracing a prehistoric ocean shoreline. Northward, pine trees stand sentinel along the Piedmont's rocky hillsides. To the south and east, the sandy Coastal Plain eases toward the Atlantic. The Fall Line also marks where maritime and continental climates meet, keeping skies clear two-thirds of the year and maintaining an annual temperature near 65°F.

Bibb County residents can find recreation and relaxation at many scenic areas. Photo by Ken Krakow

Mild weather, a beautifully variegated landscape and rich soil apparently appealed to prehistoric tribes; for nearly 12,000 years, people have gathered along the banks of the Ocmulgee River. Paleo-Indians arrived sometime before 9000 B.C., perhaps hunting the last big game of the Ice Age. They left behind spear points on the Macon Plateau, an area of fertile soil near present-day Macon. Archaeological excavations suggest people have continually inhabited the area since then.

Between A.D. 900 and 1200, a group of Native Americans linked to the Early Mississippians domesticated the Macon Plateau, now known as the Ocmulgee Old Fields, and gave the area lasting landmarks. Inside their terraced village, these skillful farmers grew corn, beans, sunflowers, and other staples. Their relics indicate they stored enough food to enjoy recreational activities. The Early Mississipians also spent time on construction projects. They built an earthen ceremonial center with lodges, temples, and burial mounds.

Three miles down the Ocmulgee River, archaeologists have identified a second village they call Lamar. This significant site was inhabited by Late Mississippians, who, like their predecessors, constructed earthen mounds. One structure features an ingenious spiral ramp ascending the mound, an archaeological treasure unlike any other still standing in the United States.

The National Park Service operates the Ocmulgee National Monument today, including the Ocmulgee Old Fields and the Lamar site. Founded in 1936, the Ocmulgee National Monument offers an interpretive center, walking trails, excavation sites, preserved mounds, and other archaeological traces of the area's extensive history. Ocmulgee Old Fields, perhaps the site of the country's first "convention" center, encompasses some 700 acres just outside of Macon—and only minutes from the contemporary Macon convention center, the Macon Centreplex.

TODAY'S MEETING PLACE

The Macon Centreplex incorporates all the advanced technology of a modern meeting facility, yet embraces traditional Southern hospitality. A superbly functional design combines the Macon

• One of downtown's most impressive landmarks is the Bibb County Courthouse, located on the corner of Mulberry and Second streets.
Photo by Ken Krakow

Coliseum and Edgar H. Wilson Convention Centre, offering 120,000 square feet under one roof. The Convention Centre, built in 1996, features gracious rotunda lobbies and a spacious floor plan. Highly versatile, the facility easily accommodates corporate functions of all sizes, as well as exhibitions, banquets, and other gatherings.

Renovations completed in 1996 at the Macon Coliseum complement the Convention Centre's appealingly open architecture. The original facility, built in 1968, was the first of its size and type in the state, according to the Macon-Bibb County Convention and Visitors Bureau. Audiences from across the region have welcomed big-name performers such as Elvis, Billy Joel, Reba McEntire, and Elton John; conventions, circuses, and sporting events of all types also have attracted audiences to fill the 9,282 seats.

As part of the Macon Centreplex operations, the historic Macon City Auditorium offers a premier venue for events, ceremonies, and performances. Formidable Greek Doric limestone columns line the sweeping terraces beneath the world's largest unsupported copper-covered dome. The Mormon Tabernacle in Salt Lake City supposedly inspired the building's architects.

Thanks to multimillion-dollar renovations in the late 1970s and again in the 1990s, the building retains its original 1925 appearance while providing enhanced safety, comfort, and functionality. A historic landmark listed in the National Register of Historic Places, the Macon City Auditorium offers seating for more than 2,600, or 14,000 square feet of exhibition space in the circular Great Hall. A beautiful 60-foot-wide mural by Don Carlos Dubois and Wilbur Kurtz adorns the stage opening. The artwork traces the area's history from the arrival of Hernando DeSoto in 1540 through World War I.

• Visitors can explore Macon's many possibilities for sightseeing at two Welcome Centers, one on I-75 south and the other on Cherry Street downtown. Photos by Ken Krakow

• (above and right) The Macon Centreplex provides accommodations for hundreds of events each year, including sports, concerts, and conventions. Photos by Ken Krakow

The Macon Centreplex, the state's largest convention and entertainment center outside of Atlanta, schedules more than 1,000 events each year. From famous musicians to massive exhibitions, the list of events and performances draws people from all over the state and the nation to Macon.

TRAVELING TO MACON

Unlike the earliest visitors to Macon who arrived on foot, today's travelers drive a bustling freeway with several lanes of fast-flowing traffic. The main north-south thoroughfare, I-75, simplifies driving anywhere in Macon. The east-west routes include I-16, connecting Macon to Savannah, and the Fall Line Freeway, also called the Eisenhower Parkway. In addition, I-475 skirts the city; four U.S. highways and eight state highways also serve Macon. When guests ask how long it will take to travel from Point A to Point B, the standard answer is "twenty minutes." In truth, that's about all the time it takes!

Macon's convenient location, quite literally at the center of the state, makes it an accessible destination. More than two-thirds of Georgia's population can drive to Macon in about an hour. And it takes no more than four hours to drive from Macon to the Gulf of Mexico, just under three hours to reach the Atlantic Ocean, and

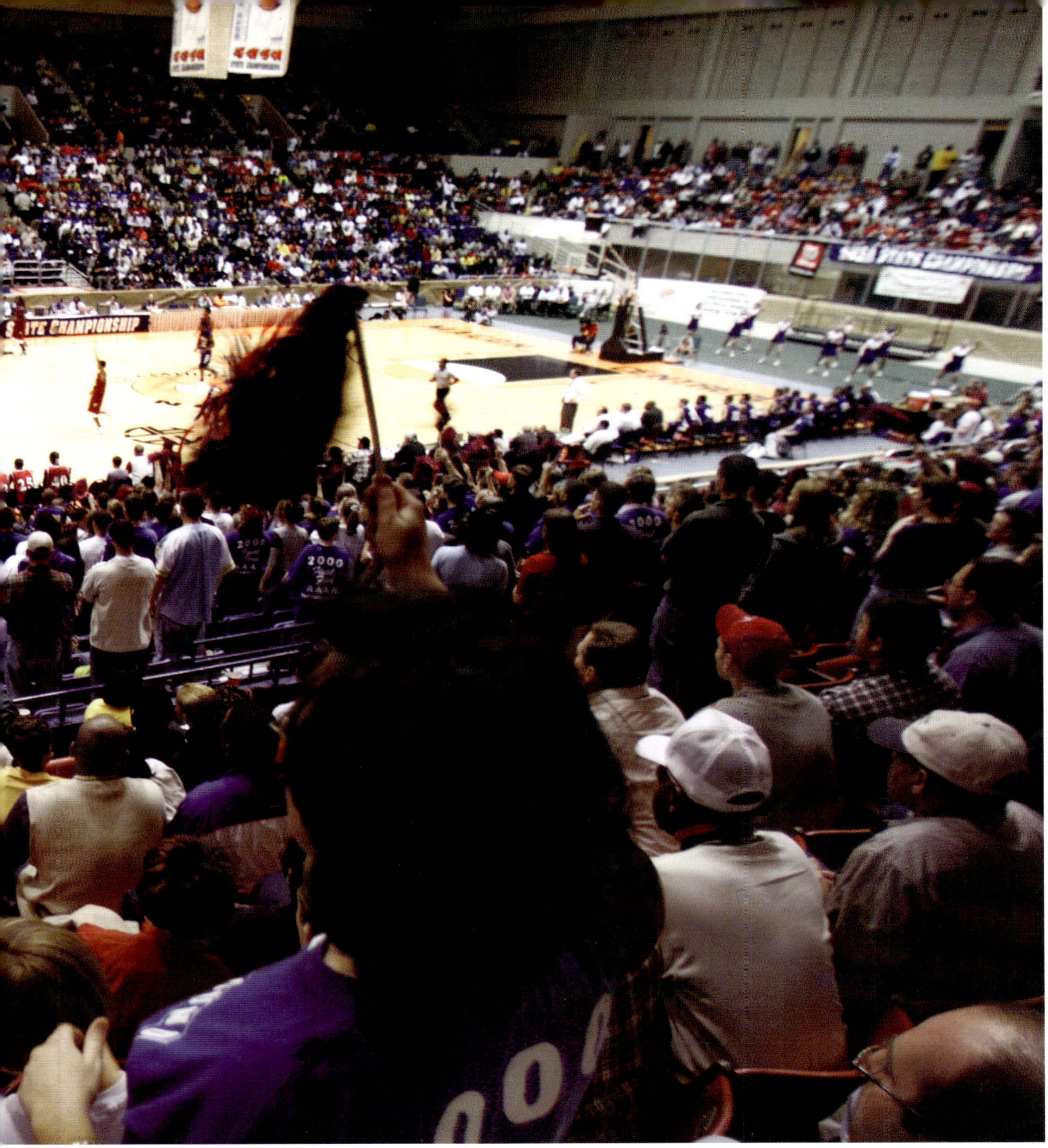
STATE CHAMPIONSHIP

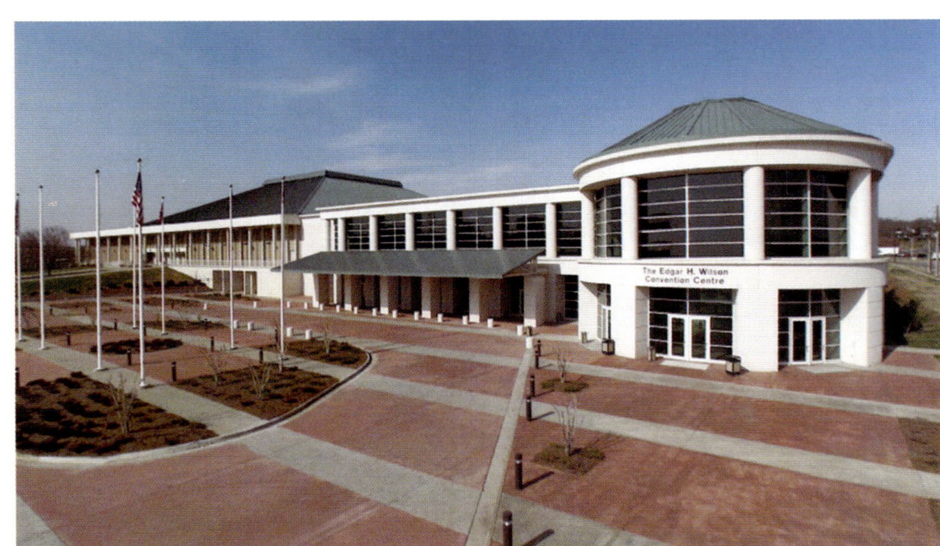

The Edgar H. Wilson
Convention Centre

• Antebellum mansions, part of Bibb County's rich cultural heritage, still exist in abundance. Photo by Ken Krakow

barely over an hour to arrive in Atlanta. Guests also may arrive via commercial air service at the Middle Georgia Regional Airport or the Herbert Smart Airport.

Thousands of travelers stop every year at the beautiful Welcome Center north of Macon off I-75. The hosts and hostesses at the Welcome Center knowledgeably dispense local information, such as directions to popular attractions or recommendations for a picnic lunch spot. Visitors receive handfuls of brochures to help them enjoy their Macon excursion.

The Macon Downtown Welcome Center in the historic Terminal Station also adeptly directs visitors to the city's many historic, entertainment, and cultural sites. The Macon-Bibb County Convention and Visitors Bureau, housed in the Terminal Station as well, books group tours, conventions, and meetings. In the 1999-2000 fiscal year, the agency assisted more than 480 conventions and 212,125 meeting delegates.

Independent research shows that tourism now contributes well over $300 million to the economy for Macon and Bibb County. About 12 percent of the area's jobs relate to tourism as well. Many of those jobs are within the hospitality industry, including employment at more than twenty meeting hotels. Approximately 4,000 guest rooms in the area help ensure that visitors have a place to rest after a long day of sightseeing.

Location alone certainly draws people to Macon, whether it's the convenience of the freeway, the South's prized antebellum mansions, or the breathtaking scenery along the Fall Line. Indeed, Macon's central location continues to underscore the city's momentum, providing a premier setting for economic development, cultural enrichment, and recreational opportunities—a place for progress mindful of the past. ❋

• (right) Items used hundreds of years ago by the Mississippian culture can be viewed at Ocmulgee National Monument, established in 1934. The site contains some of the most significant artifacts of this American Indian group, also known as Mound Builders. Photo by Ken Krakow

• (below) Archaeologists supervise excavation at Ocmulgee National Monument in 1936, shortly after the area received federal designation for its historical treasures. Photo courtesy of the Middle Georgia Archives

BROWN & WILLIAMSON TOBACCO CORPORATION

Brown & Williamson, an international leader in the cigarette manufacturing industry, has been an indispensable part of the Macon community since 1977. It is one of Middle Georgia's largest private employers, contributing almost $500 million a year to the state's economy and $1 million to charitable agencies and organizations.

Its Macon complex, with 54 acres under roof, contains manufacturing operations as well as several corporate functions, and the most advanced machinery and technology within the industry, including its own power plant and wastewater treatment facility.

But Brown & Williamson is more than just a manufacturing giant. The company is dedicated to the principles of safety, quality, performance, and community, providing only the best to its employees, customers, and neighbors.

CENTRAL GEORGIA HEALTH SYSTEM

Central Georgia Health System serves as a parent company over several entities, including The Medical Center of Central Georgia, the largest health-care facility in this region.

The Medical Center's mission is to enhance the health status of those it serves in partnership with medical staff and community organizations by providing wellness services, health education and training, and access to high-quality health care.

• Photos by Ken Krakow

COLISEUM HEALTH SYSTEM

Coliseum Health System is a three-hospital network comprised of Coliseum Medical Centers, Macon Northside Hospital, and Middle Georgia Hospital. All three full-service medical-surgical hospitals create an important dimension of health care in the Middle Georgia area.

Coliseum Medical Centers, a 258-bed facility located near downtown Macon, provides a full range of services including a birthing center, psychiatric center, breast health center, and metabolic center. Macon Northside Hospital, Macon's newest hospital, is a 103-bed neighborhood hospital that provides a 24-hour emergency-room service and is conveniently located close to many residential, shopping, and school areas. Located in the heart of historic downtown Macon, Middle Georgia Hospital is a 119-bed facility offering quality medical and surgical inpatient and outpatient services, as well as a Wound Healing Center and a geno-psychiatric program.

• Photos by Ken Krakow

IKON OFFICE SOLUTIONS AND IOS CAPITAL

IKON Office Solutions' Business Services Division began in Middle Georgia with the acquisition of Acme Business Products in 1983. The home office for the Southern Marketplace, still located in Macon, manages more than 15 branch locations in four different states. A worldwide business communications solutions provider, IKON's Business Services Division provides its customers "total solutions" for the effective communication of their business information.

IOS Capital, formerly Alco Capital, established in 1987, provides lease financing for the customers of IKON Office Solutions, one of the world's leading providers of business communications products and services. A full leasing company, IOS Capital's functions range from credit, contract review, billing, customer service, collections, and asset recovery, to supporting IKON's national accounts.

• Photos by Ken Krakow

MACON CENTREPLEX

Macon's award-winning, state-of-the-art, multi-purpose convention and entertainment facility, the Macon Centreplex, is Georgia's largest convention/event venue outside of metro-Atlanta. Since the completion of the $20-million construction and renovation project in 1996, which added the Edgar H. Wilson Convention Centre, the Centreplex has more than doubled its event numbers.

The Macon Centreplex is actually comprised of three facilities: the Macon Coliseum and the adjoining Convention Centre, located near the intersection of I-75 and I-16, and the beautiful Macon City Auditorium—listed on the National Register of Historic Places—located in the heart of the historic district of downtown Macon. The three facilities host events ranging from small gatherings to large conventions, concerts, and sporting events.

MERCER UNIVERSITY

Macon is proud to be home to one of the South's premiere institutions of higher learning. Mercer University has had a unique relationship with the city since the University moved from Penfield, Georgia, to Macon in 1871. From its earliest days, Mercer has been committed to serving the community.

Today, Mercer has campuses in Macon and Atlanta. It meets the educational and research needs of the region through nine academic programs—liberal arts, law, pharmacy, medicine, business, engineering, education, theology, and nursing.

Mercer contributes to Macon educationally, economically, and culturally. From the Executive Forum business enrichment program to leadership in the downtown redevelopment effort to management of the historic Grand Opera House, Mercer continues to flourish with its roots planted deeply in Macon.

CHAPTER TWO

2

Bounty from the Earth

The soil surrounding Macon became a source for prosperity in the 1800s as King Cotton reigned supreme. Contemporary Macon still sees agricultural influences within the local economy, including processing facilities for tobacco, wood, and farm products. The kaolin industry also grew from the earth's bounty here.

Photo by Ken Krakow

• (top) The city of Macon is named for Nathaniel Macon, a statesman and soldier from North Carolina. Photo courtesy of the Middle Georgia Archives

• (above) A reconstructed blockhouse marks the site of Fort Benjamin Hawkins, which served as an Army supply base during the War of 1812. Photo by Ken Krakow

When Hernando DeSoto arrived near the Macon site in 1540, he discovered Hitchiti Native Americans growing maize and other staple foods along the fertile plateau. Historians believe the Hitchiti and Muscogees, or Creeks as the English later named them, blended together after the Muscogees arrived from their homelands beyond the Mississippi River. The rich soil the Muscogees found near the Ocmulgee River allowed them to end their travels and establish a thriving town.

The same fertile soil later attracted the first white settlers to the area. Cotton farming started in Georgia in the early 1730s, but this row crop did not take root in the local economy and culture until after the turn of the century.

In 1807, soldiers arrived at Fort Hawkins on the Ocmulgee River's eastern bank to protect America's frontier bordering the Muscogee Confederacy. The enhanced security drew civilians, especially farmers. They called their settlement outside the fort "New Town" or "Newtown," although the name "Fort Hawkins" also remained in use long after the fort's military role ceased in 1818. A replica blockhouse honors the original fort site today.

Area farmers first sent their cotton downstream from Macon in 1817, six years before the city was established. Old Federal Road, now aptly named Cotton Avenue, also predates Macon. This early freight route ran diagonally across the grid of city streets to reduce cornering for bulky cotton wagons destined for the docks.

As wharf traffic grew, so did the local population. Georgia's legislature officially created Bibb County in 1822, named for U.S. Senator William Wyatt Bibb. Macon, named in honor of North Carolina statesman and soldier Nathaniel Macon, became the county seat.

That same year, the fledgling community began as a planned development. City fathers envisioned wide avenues with names of the forest trees intersected by numbered streets. Refreshing parks anchored their spacious plan. Lots were sold at auction, and construction began. In just two months' time, seventeen structures rose. Many of them were warehouses for cotton.

This new cotton-market town received its formal induction to the cotton trade when the steamboat *Pioneer* docked here in 1833. Grand city retreats for plantation owners and other stately mansions reflected King Cotton's supremacy. Despite the Civil War and Reconstruction's upheaval, cotton continued to exert a strong influence on the local economy and culture well into the 1900s.

STILL GROWING STRONG

Macon's role in the cotton industry dwindled when the Ocmulgee River proved unfeasible to navigate and railroads expanded their prominence. Cotton itself began an unexpected fall from grace when the devastating boll weevil began eating into farmers' profits in 1914. Over the next several decades, many farmers switched to peanuts or other crops, or they gave up entirely. From a record high of 5.2 million acres planted in 1914, Georgia's cotton hit a record low of 120,000 acres planted in 1983. But a Boll Weevil Eradication Program begun in 1987 helped rekindle cotton farming, making cotton the state's biggest row crop commodity today.

The land continues to support farm families and enhance the local economy. Large stands of Georgia's famous peaches grow near Macon, helping to keep the state among the country's top three peach producers. Approximately 3,000 acres of peaches and 1,500 acres of pecans grow under the practiced hands of Lane Packing Company, a fourth-generation family farm near Fort Valley. Begun in 1908, the firm now operates one of the world's most advanced packing facilities and enjoys global acclaim for its retail, mail-order, and Internet business. The company's Roadside Market first opened in 1990. Offering tours, fresh pickings, and other tasty treats, the Roadside Market ranks as one of the area's top attractions.

Not surprisingly, the state selected nearby Perry for the Georgia National Fairgrounds & Agricenter. More than 1,000 beautifully landscaped acres adorned with lakes, gardens, and exhibition facilities showcase livestock and horse shows, fairs, and other family and agri-business events. The state-sponsored Georgia National Fair opens here in autumn, too. Reflecting the area's agricultural influences, the center's mission focuses on promoting education and awareness for agriculture and agri-businesses.

The State Farmers Market on Eisenhower Parkway also highlights the growing success of area farmers. Truckloads of delicious fresh fruits and vegetables fill the long stalls, especially on weekends in summer and early fall.

INDUSTRY ROOTED IN AGRICULTURE

Vestiges of the area's agricultural heritage echo among many of the key industries encircling Macon. The textile industries, close kin to the cotton industries, found success in Macon. Most were smaller businesses until 1972, when YKK Corporation of America selected Macon's Ocmulgee Industrial Park for its new facility. Today, the world's largest zipper manufacturing company employs more than 1,000 people here. A vertically integrated system of twelve plants

• In the 1800s, the cotton trade flourished in Macon and became the city's economic mainstay. During the 1900s, however, the area's cotton crop dwindled when fields became infested with the destructive boll weevil. Today, cotton has made a comeback, thanks to a Boll Weevil Eradication Program begun in 1987.

(top) Photo by Ken Krakow

(left) Photo courtesy of the Middle Georgia Archives

produces the necessary materials, from 99.98 percent pure brass zipper teeth and sliders to custom-dyed thread. The facility offers 1,500 zipper styles in 427 standard colors. Some seven million zippers receive the globally renowned YKK stamp every day in Macon.

Ocmulgee Industrial Park was developed from remnants of the 11,500-acre Camp Wheeler, a significant military training facility during World War I and World War II. The exceptionally clean and well-maintained Ocmulgee Industrial Park covers about 1,500 acres. After YKK Corporation of America built its facilities, several other textile-related firms, such as Texprint (Ga.), Inc., moved to Ocmulgee Industrial Park, too.

Another significant employer with agricultural ties took notice of Macon's Ocmulgee Industrial Park not long after YKK. Brown & Williamson Tobacco Corporation found the city's central location in the Southeastern tobacco region especially appealing. Cooperative efforts with local and state officials convinced Brown & Williamson to relocate in 1976. The company's highly sophisticated fabrication facility crowns 200 acres in Ocmulgee Industrial Park. By 2000, this internationally recognized cigarette manufacturer counted more than 2,900 workers in Macon and ranked as a top-ten employer.

• From farmland to corporate offices, Macon's ties to agriculture remain strong. The headquarters for Brown & Williamson Tobacco Corporation, right, is located in Macon, and the company is among the area's top employers. Photos by Ken Krakow

SUCCESS FROM THE GROUND UP

The prehistoric ocean left behind more than fossilized shark teeth and sand dollars near Macon. Beneath the Fall Line, the world's largest known kaolin deposit formed from the erosion and pressure of the ancient seas. Kaolin, a crumbly white clay, undergoes an extensive refining process before it becomes a key ingredient for manufacturing paper, paint, ink, adhesives, rubber, pharmaceuticals, plastics, and even toothpaste. Some people call it china clay since it's also used for fine porcelains and ceramics.

Kaolin mining began along the Fall Line in the 1920s. Today some 4,200 Georgians work directly for kaolin mining companies such as Engelhard Corporation, Dry Branch Kaolin Company, J. M. Huber Corporation, Thiele Kaolin Company, and ECC International. The China Clay Producers Association reports that kaolin's economic impact to middle Georgia surpasses $150 million annually.

More impressive still, kaolin's versatility in manufacturing and close proximity has spurred several businesses in the Macon area. Burgess Pigment Company, headquartered off Pierce Avenue, processes thousands of tons of kaolin every year at its Washington County facility. Armstrong World Industries relies on a steady supply of locally refined kaolin to manufacture commercial and residential ceilings. Riverwood International Georgia similarly uses kaolin—about 38,700 tons annually—to produce more than 495,000 tons of quality paperboard.

Ready access to ample timber, not kaolin, initially brought both Armstrong World Industries and Riverwood International Georgia to the Allied Industrial Park just south of downtown Macon. Today, these industrial neighbors now employ more than 1,000 people. An additional 1,000-plus workers at companies such as diaper maker

• By the 1940s, kaolin mining had become a lucrative business in Bibb County. The white, clay-like substance is a key ingredient in a variety of products, including paper, paint, and fine porcelain. Several industries have located in the area to take advantage of kaolin's abundance and proximity. At the facilities of Riverwood International Georgia, right, kaolin is used to produce quality paperboard.

(right) Photo by Ken Krakow

(below) Photo courtesy of the Middle Georgia Archives

Paragon Trade Brands, Bassett Furniture Industries, wood specialty company Bilco Manufacturing Corporation, and Mil-Spec Packaging of Georgia, Inc., also reflect the economic impact of the forests and other natural resources surrounding Macon.

Timber ranks as one of Georgia's top crops, along with livestock and poultry. Cagles, Inc., employs some 450 people to process chicken in Macon. Pactiv packaging, also in Macon, puts another 240 people to work making egg cartons. Other food-related firms in the vicinity, such as Keebler Company, Earth Grains Baking Company, and Frito Lay underscore the keen relationship between industry and agriculture as well. ❋

• J. M. Huber Corporation, an international supplier of kaolin, maintains mining operations near Macon. Photo by Ken Krakow

CHAPTER THREE

3

Commerce Commences

Within seven years of its formal incorporation, Macon began defining itself as a regional trading center. A visitor in 1830 wrote that she found Macon to be "the most flourishing, wealthy, and polite town, to the age of it, in the United States." Commerce found a foothold along the wide avenues near the Ocmulgee River, and soon merchants, bankers, and hoteliers ranked among the city's prosperous citizens.

In the 1800s, Macon gained prominence as a commercial center, and the area's wealthiest citizens built opulent mansions. Woodruff House, constructed in 1836, was occupied by Union forces in 1865.
Photo by Ken Krakow

Then, as now, the *Macon Telegraph* provided a written record of the busy community's affairs. Founded as a weekly paper in 1826, the newspaper began publishing daily in 1831. Its modern offices and upgraded production facility reflect the continued success of the downtown business area.

While many businesses of those early decades have disappeared over time, several buildings constructed then still stand. Their changing tenants often reflected the city's evolution from a frontier town to a thriving marketplace. Of these many historic buildings, Macon City Hall aptly chronicles the ongoing transformation. The Monroe Railroad and Banking Company established offices in this impressive building overlooking the city in 1838. The business fell into bankruptcy, but an enterprising Maconite purchased it. The distinctive structure became Macon's first fireproof cotton warehouse, protecting 6,000 bales in fine style!

The city bought the building in 1860, and it soon became a hospital for injured soldiers during the Civil War. The state government temporarily worked in the building in 1864, when the capitol building at nearby Milledgeville was threatened by Union troops. Later the structure resumed its professional status when it became Macon City Hall. Remodeling in 1904 added wings and a pediment, and further renovation occurred over the years. In 1999, a $1.7-million construction project began to create Civic Square, a park-like pedestrian connector between City Hall and the City Auditorium. In addition to improving traffic flow, Civic Square reconfirmed the city's commitment to preserving an inviting atmosphere downtown.

PROGRESS IN PRESERVING THE PAST

An invigorating sense of renewal, conceived from a blend of historical reverence and progressive opportunity, seems to emanate from Macon's downtown today. Like so many other urban centers in the United States, Macon faced declining activity when suburbs gained popularity in the middle part of the 20th century. The city's bustling downtown of the '60s faded during the '70s and early '80s. However, the foresight and ingenuity that characterized Macon's early years resurfaced as citizens confronted this multifaceted issue.

Business owners, downtown workers, and residents assessed the possibilities. Because Macon escaped Civil War damage, many antebellum homes and commercial structures still lined city streets. An opportunity to combine downtown revitalization with tourism, cultural awareness, and enhanced aesthetic appeal reinforced the dawning preservation effort.

The Middle Georgia Historical Society, established in 1964, led the movement and achieved dramatic results in the 1970s, including restoration of the Grand Opera House and the Macon City Auditorium. The group, housed in the Sidney Lanier Cottage, remains strongly committed to historic preservation. Members focus on educational programs and serve as resources for anyone interested in Macon's historic buildings.

The Macon Heritage Foundation, a consortium created by the Middle Georgia Historical Society and the Intown Macon Neighborhood Association, has assumed more of the brick-and-mortar duties of the local preservation movement. The group worked diligently for approval of the Historic Zoning Ordinance in the '70s,

• Revitilization efforts by many Macon citizens have led to restoration of charming homes in the downtown area.
Photo by Ken Krakow

protecting the city's charming ambiance for future generations. The Macon Heritage Foundation is another vital community resource. This group has helped more than 300 property owners obtain tax credits or tax abatement advantages for rehabilitating historic structures.

DOWNTOWN REJUVENATION CONTINUES

While the grassroots preservation movement gained momentum, city leaders sought a complementary approach to rejuvenate the downtown area. During the 1980s, some eighty buildings received significant upgrades as a result of incentives offered through the local government. Others followed. Large-scale renovation projects have included Douglass Theatre, Georgia Children's Museum, Goodwill Emporium, Medical Center of Central Georgia, Lawrence Mayer Florist, the Bankruptcy Court of the U.S. Judiciary Department, and the Macon Heritage Foundation.

The city's enhanced image in the 1990s rekindled interest among retailers, too. Some businesses moved here from other states, and entrepreneurs also revived companies that had roots in the area. The Karsten-Denson Company hardware store, established in 1917, found new life in a rehabilitated auto dealership building. The Greater Macon Chamber of Commerce, founded more than 130 years ago, renovated its 30-year-old facility in 1999. Several newly constructed buildings, such as the Peyton Anderson Community Services Center and the in-town Kroger grocery store, incorporated specific architectural elements to merge with the historic landscape, too.

The visionary plan implemented by civic leaders features beautifully landscaped pedestrian plazas to link various retail, office, hospitality, and museum buildings. Of these, the fountain park facing the Georgia Music Hall of Fame has become a new favorite. Music notes dance along the edges of the towering sculpture, a piece shaped to resemble the Hall of Fame's annual Georgie Award statue. Bubbling water leaps up to the music-staff wall and plays its own relaxing tune.

• (above) In 1838 Monroe Railroad and Banking Company built an impressive office in downtown Macon, but the company fell into bankruptcy and was forced to sell the building. Through the years, it served as a cotton warehouse, a Confederate hospital, and finally as Macon City Hall. By the early 1900s, the landmark structure had undergone major renovations. Photo courtesy of the Middle Georgia Archives

• (below) Karsten-Denson Company was established in Macon more than 80 years ago. When the company needed a new home, owners opted to renovate an older downtown building. Photo by Ken Krakow

• (top) GEICO, which employs more than 3,500 area residents, moved into a new facility at Ocmulgee Industrial Park in late 1999.

• (right) When the workday is over, Maconites can unwind with a range of recreational pursuits. Photos by Ken Krakow

Indeed, Macon has rightfully reclaimed its 19th century moniker, "A City in a Park," counting more than thirty acres of meticulously maintained parks inside the city limits. The Parks and Recreation Department manages about 1,550 acres in Bibb County as well. Twice each year the dedicated team plants 8,000 flowers along city streets and in parks, adding even more vibrance to the area.

SUCCESS ALL AROUND THE CITY

Macon's continuing success reflects a commitment to sustainable jobs and sensible development, whether for downtown or in suburban areas. Elected officials work in concert with organizations such as the Greater Macon Chamber of Commerce, the Macon Economic Development Commission (MEDC), the Macon-Bibb County Industrial Authority, the Downtown Council, the Urban Development Authority and the Development Authority of Bibb County to attract and maintain viable businesses.

Job growth at the start of the second millennium, particularly strong among finance, insurance, real estate, and other back-office sectors, has stimulated new construction projects beyond downtown's land capacity. Many companies simply outgrew their original facilities.

At the start of the 1990s, GEICO (Government Employees Insurance Company) operated one building on eight acres in Ocmulgee East Industrial Park. In late 1999, some of the 3,500 employees began moving into a newly constructed 235,000-square-foot facility on an expanded 150-acre campus. The additional space also will help house 1,500 more people expected to join the company's workforce before 2005.

IKON Office Solutions, a major office product and service provider, also chose Macon for a recent expansion. In 1997, IKON already employed 350 people for data management and leasing operations. At the time, however, the company had only four employees at its Macon Shared Service Center. Three years later, IKON expected that number to reach 225, pushing the total Macon workforce toward 575 and filling four large office buildings.

Similarly, Georgia Farm Bureau Federation increased its workforce by 100 people to 480 in the years between 1995 and 2000. In 1941 the state headquarters opened in Macon with 1,313 members. Today more than 322,540 members statewide rely on the insurance, investment, real estate, and other services offered by the organization.

Several other back-office businesses have flourished in Macon as well. GE Capital Credit Services, an account-processing center, employs some 400 workers. The impressive Wal-Mart Return Center also maintains a workforce of about 425. A new Wal-Mart "Super Store," which opened in 2000 along Gray Highway, complements the Wal-Mart operational presence here and reflects the booming retail sector.

THE STATE'S SHOPPING CENTER

Macon's convenient central location has attracted shoppers from across the region for decades. Shoppers from a thirty-county radius began appearing regularly in Macon when the Westgate Center opened in 1961. Westgate Mall, as it was originally named, featured the state's first enclosed, climate-controlled shopping experience. The center shifted its focus, however, with changes in the local retail environment. Wal-Mart moved to the site in 1987. A complete renovation followed in 1994, creating the current strip-mall design with about 300,000 square feet of additional retail space. Big-name stores, including Home Depot and Media Play, helped position Westgate Center as one of the most heavily shopped retail complexes in central Georgia, second only to Colonial Mall Macon.

• (top) The 400-seat Douglass Theatre underwent a major renovation in 1997. Many great African-American entertainers launched their careers at the Douglass, including Otis Redding and Little Richard.
Photo by Woody Marshall

• (left) Shoppers can select from 200 stores at Colonial Mall Macon, the largest shopping center in central Georgia.
Photo by Ken Krakow

• (right) In the 1800s, Macon earned a reputation for its lovely parks. Residents in 1876 enjoy Central City Park's May 1st celebration.

• (below) Baby Boomers might recall cruising on the train through Ragans Park in the 1950s. Photos courtesy of the Middle Georgia Archives

Colonial Mall Macon, now Georgia's largest enclosed mall with thirty acres of stores, has proven itself to be an irresistible destination for travelers from across the state. The mall first opened in 1975. A major expansion, completed in the late 1990s, made it one of few malls worldwide that has six department stores. Approximately 200 stores and thirty eateries covering 1.6 million square feet dazzle shoppers beneath spectacular skylights.

Beyond the Eisenhower Parkway retail corridor, abundant shopping opportunities exist throughout Macon. Specialty stores downtown complement the variety of merchandise offered at several area strip-malls. Well-positioned in newly developed areas from Bass Road and Tom Hill Sr. Boulevard on the northside to the Hartley Bridge Road area on the southern fringe, these collections of stores aptly reflect Macon's continuing growth. ❋

• Whether racing to find Easter eggs, or strolling through cherry blossoms, visitors will find a great escape in Macon's parks.

(top) Photo by Beau Campbell

(right) Photo by Sherry DiBari

TERMINAL
STATION
MCMXVI

CHAPTER FOUR

4

Made in Macon

Today, the Ocmulgee River slowly sashays through Macon, giving few clues to its historic role in the city's development. In the late 1820s and early 1830s, hundreds of thousands of cotton bales left the port of Macon on barges and steamships. The river provided a vital link to other markets, such as coastal Darien, and secured the city's future in trade.

Terminal Station opened in 1916, and Macon became a hub for passenger and freight transportation. The restored train station is home to one of the city's two Welcome Centers. Photo by Ken Krakow

Changes in steamship design and improvements in railroad systems brought Macon to a critical crossroad. The community boldly chose to shift away from river traffic and looked to the promise of rail instead; in 1833, Macon chartered the state's first railway. Five years later, Georgia's first train, the Ocmulgee, arrived in Macon.

The daring venture into railroad shipping set the stage for Macon's growth well into the next century. Passenger and freight trains from more than ten railroad lines regularly rumbled into the city, stopping at their own company depots. The Union Station, now known as Terminal Station, created a central passenger depot to simplify connections. Built in 1916, this impressive landmark sometimes saw more than 100 trains a day.

Inside Terminal Station, a catwalk suspended above the mesmerizing commotion became a favorite lookout for children. Even today, visitors standing in the great hall can easily understand the fascination this place must have held for all of Macon.

Passenger rail service, last seen in the 1970s, has generated renewed interest in recent years. High-speed service between Macon and Atlanta in particular offers tremendous economic potential for the entire central Georgia region.

Still a significant component in Macon's transportation network, freight trains efficiently connect the city with the entire Southeast. The Brosnan Yard skirts the edge of downtown and is a major rail classification yard for Norfolk Southern Company. Locally, Norfolk Southern serves the seaports of Savannah and Brunswick, Georgia, and hauls raw materials and finished products in all directions from Macon.

• In the early 1900s, steamboats still chugged along the Ocmulgee River, carrying passengers and cargo.
Photo courtesy of the Middle Georgia Archives

CENTERED ON THE FREEWAYS

The railroad hasn't been the only major transportation system to benefit from Macon's often progressive leadership. When the national interstate system began redefining America's travel in the early 1960s, the I-75 freeway nearly missed Macon. Reginald Trice Parkway, a section of I-75, honors the man who paved the way for the interstate to come through Macon.

Today, I-75, I-16, and I-475 help maximize Macon's accessibility. The variety of trucking and warehousing firms here attests to the city's strength as a distribution hub. Macon is headquarters for the United States Postal Service South Georgia District, and employees process more than a million pieces of mail each day. GIGA, Inc., a procurement enterprise for government and industry, sends merchandise shipments around the globe from its facility in Airport Industrial Park. Similarly, the Saddle Creek Corporation processes an average of 100 trucks every day at its 897,000-square-foot plant in Ocmulgee East Industrial Park. The company provides warehousing, transportation, and integrated logistics for clients throughout the Southeast.

Macon remains committed to improving its highway system. Plans call for freeway connectors and other significant projects well into the second decade of the new millennium.

FUELING MACON'S GROWTH

Complementing the transportation infrastructure, area utility providers ensure that ample and affordable resources exist for continued industrial and residential growth. Major natural gas pipelines run through Macon and Bibb County. In addition, Electric Membership Corporations (EMCs), which were created in the 1930s to deliver power to rural customers, continue to efficiently serve areas outside metropolitan Macon. Not-for-profit entities in the region include Flint, Tri-County, Central Georgia, Lamar, and Oconee electric membership corporations. Georgia customers requiring loads of 900 KW or greater may choose service from EMCs, municipal power systems, or investor-owned utilities.

Georgia Power, part of Southern Company, also provides energy solutions to business and residential customers here. Formed in 1883 in Atlanta, the company now powers all but six of the state's 159 counties. The company employs 8,300 statewide, including the experts of Georgia Power Economic Development.

Georgia Power Economic Development offers confidential turnkey guidance to businesses that might move to the state. Services include engineering and technical expertise, and the company also offers free assistance to clients through an extensive database at the Georgia Resource Center.

To construct a new business park in the late 1990s, the Macon Economic Development Commission worked closely with the Georgia Power Economic Development team, an international site selection firm, and representatives from the Georgia Department of Industry Trade and Tourism (GDITT). Encompassing 456 acres along two miles of freeway, the I-75 Business Park especially appeals to high-tech manufacturers.

TECHNICALLY SUPPORTIVE

Understanding that economic growth and industrial development rely upon state-of-the-art capabilities, Macon's utility companies have readily embraced technological advances. Tremendous Internet developments during the late 1990s especially focused attention on telecommunications and other technology-based firms. Among them, BellSouth Telecommunications, Inc., ranks as one of the largest employers, with a workforce of 700. The company provides a full range of services to more than 100,000 access lines for residential and commercial customers. BellSouth also tailors telecom solutions for businesses, such as electronic commerce and managed networks. The company maintains 17,500 miles of fiber-optic cable lines in the area, linking all of Macon to the world.

Cox Communications also integrates fiber-optic cable lines in its grid covering Bibb, Jones, Houston, and Peach counties as well as Robins Air Force Base. Cox Enterprises began more than 100 years ago and has grown into one of the country's largest broadband communications companies with video, voice, and data services. In fact, in 1997 Cox became the first cable system to deliver all of these services via a single broadband network of coaxial and fiber-optic cable. Within the last few years, Cox Digital Cable launched Cox@Home to offer residential customers enhanced Internet performance with CD-quality sound and constant accessibility.

• Railways expanded quickly as the 20th century began, and the Central of Georgia Railroad shop always stayed busy. Photo courtesy of the Middle Georgia Archives

• Georgia Power, part of Southern Company, plays a vital role in meeting Macon's electricity needs. Electric Membership Corporations also serve Bibb County by providing power to residents in rural areas.
Photo by Ken Krakow

TECHNOLOGY MIXES WITH WATER

Ever a basic necessity, water is hardly a simple matter today. State-of-the-art technology helps ensure purity and capacity for Macon's water under the guidance of the Macon Water Authority. This public utility corporation oversees water mains and service lines covering some 1,425 miles and a sewer system running about 1,360 miles.

The historic flood of 1994, which sent the Ocmulgee River more than three feet above the 500-year flood projections, revised the Macon Water Authority's long-term plans for its in-town plant. Instead, the Macon Water Authority built a completely new facility on 3,000 acres next to the Town Creek Reservoir in Jones County. The Town Creek Water Treatment facility, operational at the millennium, features a capacity of 60 million gallons per day with expansion possibilities for 90 MGD. Just as impressive, plans for the surrounding property include a recreational area for hiking, biking, and fishing.

The new water facility reinforces Macon's sound existing infrastructure. The reliable utilities here have helped generate a diversified industrial base. Some companies, such as Cherokee Brick & Tile Company, Blue Bird Bus Corporation, and Bearings and Drives, Inc., began in or around Macon. Other firms with large workforces moved here over time, including the Trane Company and Bassett Furniture Industries. From roofing products to recycled metals, a vast array of products now ships from Macon manufacturers.

• With its efficient highway system, Macon supports a variety of trucking companies and serves as a center for distribution. Photo by Woody Marshall

FRIENDLY TO INDUSTRY

Macon's heritage of hospitality has adapted well to the industrial arena, welcoming employers of all kinds to the area through the years. In 1941, a particularly industry-friendly gesture by the Greater Macon Chamber of Commerce and the city of Macon changed the economic picture for all of Middle Georgia. These two entities purchased land near Wellston Station in Houston County and donated it for the War Department to build an Army Air Depot. Wellston citizens showed their support by renaming their town "Warner Robins" to honor General Augustine Warner Robins, the new military operation's namesake.

Today, Robins Air Force Base serves several key missions. Warner Robins Air Logistics Center, the host unit on the base, carries worldwide management responsibility for the repair, modification, and overhaul of the F-15 Eagle, C-130 Hercules, C-141 Starlifter, C-5 Galaxy, and all Air Force helicopters. The center also provides logistical support for all Air Force missiles, vehicles, general purpose computers, and electronic systems for most aircraft. More than fifty units call the base home as well. The Museum of Aviation, also located at Robins Air Force Base, covers forty-three acres with indoor and outdoor exhibits.

Robins Air Force Base ranks as Georgia's largest industrial complex and contributes about $3 billion annually to the state's economy, according to the Middle Georgia Regional Development Center. Over 19,000 civil and military employees take home a net

• In the second half of the 1800s, the railway boosted industries such as Schofield Iron Works. Photos courtesy of the Middle Georgia Archives

payroll of more than $834 million. Robins Air Force Base awarded contracts totaling $2.17 billion in fiscal year 1999, with $227.1 million staying in Georgia. Impressively, numerous aerospace businesses such as TRW/Lucas Aerospace Cargo Systems, The Boeing Company, Vought Aircraft Industries, and TIMCO generate an additional 17,000 jobs in Middle Georgia and give Macon the nickname "Aerospace Alley."

Maconites take great pride in Robins Air Force Base and its accomplishments. The base's comprehensive pollution prevention program, which cut ozone-depleting solvent use, improved ambient air quality, reduced waste and saved hundreds of thousands of dollars, earned the 1999 Governor's Award for Pollution Prevention. Robins Air Force Base also pioneers innovation by working closely with local educators to encourage science and engineering programs.

Many post-secondary schools offer classes on the base. In addition, Georgia Tech maintains a branch office of its Advanced Technology Development Center at Warner Robins. The Georgia Department of Industry, Trade and Tourism also has offices in Warner Robins. Thanks to a contingent of state and local organizations, educators, and businesses, a highly qualified workforce helps Aerospace Alley soar. ❋

• In recent years, Macon's high-tech businesses have gained prominence. BellSouth Telecommunications, left, employs 700 residents and maintains 17,000 miles of fiber-optic cable in the area. The Boeing Company, below, is one of numerous aerospace businesses that have inspired a new nickname for Macon—"Aerospace Alley." Photos by Ken Krakow

RESPONSIBI
Africa South of the Sahara

CHAPTER FIVE

5

Lessons Learned

Maconites have valued education since the city's early days. Today's impressive academic opportunities range from magnet programs at local public schools to advanced studies at several area post-secondary institutions. Education and business have formed partnerships, too, creating a highly skilled workforce.

The Bibb County Public School System offers a wide range of programs that help all students achieve their academic potential. Photo by Ken Krakow

Frontier towns attracted spirited adventurers, mainly men, in the 1820s. Few children lived in Macon then and Georgia laws strictly forbade teaching slaves to read or write. Yet the early citizens saw merit in formal education. In 1824, just one year after the first city lots were sold, Bibb County Academy and a singing school opened. Lake Academy and Washington Academy enrolled pupils the following year. By 1860 a board of education existed for the county—twelve years before the state mandated "common schools."

Classes necessarily stalled during the Civil War. The Georgia Academy for the Blind, which began instruction on Orange Street in 1852, moved to Fort Valley for safety. This nationally renowned institution resumed classes in Macon in 1865 and has continuously offered specialized instruction here ever since.

Despite the economic depression constricting the South in the 1870s, schools flourished in Macon. Bibb County's Public School and Orphanage system started in 1872 and included five "Common Free Schools for Whites."

Education for blacks became legal after the end of the Civil War. Macon counted twelve schools for blacks in the 1870s—not one with enough seats for all of its students. Even by 1903, only fifty-three percent of the black children in Bibb County attended classes. Black educators stretched meager budgets and endowments to secure educational opportunities. Some, such as Minnie Smith, used personal savings to ensure formal education for black students.

A committed teacher, "Miss Minnie" founded Beda-Etta College in 1921, a school that offered business courses to black Maconites. She added a full range of subjects later and encouraged adults to take evening classes to expand their skills.

• (right) In the 1920s, students posed for a group portrait at Ballard Normal School. During the era of school segregation, African-American educators remained dedicated to helping their students succeed despite inadequate funds and facilities.

• (far right) In 1908, students and teachers in northwest Bibb County gathered for a photograph in front of Chambliss School. Photos courtesy of the Middle Georgia Archives

Segregation, entrenched throughout the South, continued in schools for another forty years. In 1964, Macon's black students began to attend formerly all-white high schools and ushered in new hope for the future.

PURSUING EXCELLENCE IN EDUCATION

Macon's early emphasis on education resounds in today's public schools, enhanced by vibrant cultural diversity and keen academic focus. More than 24,500 students attend classes at one of thirty-one elementary, five middle and five high schools in the Bibb County Public School System. Ten of these facilities feature exciting magnet programs, presenting academic choices to all Bibb County parents and students.

The first magnet school, Alexander II, began its math and science program in 1979. Alexander II was honored for its success in 1984 and 1993, when it received the School of Excellence Award from the Georgia State Department of Education. The Miller Core Knowledge Magnet School, a middle school, also received this prestigious award in 1999. In 1995 Central High School, which offers a fine arts magnet program, became the state's third traditional high school to offer the rigorous International Baccalaureate program. These and other special study courses for gifted students complement the array of educational programs designed to meet the needs of every Bibb County student.

Beyond academic choices in the public school system, parents and students may opt for one of Macon's many fine private institutions. Mount de Sales Academy, founded in 1871 by the Catholic Sisters of Mercy, began as a boarding school for girls. Today, its manicured campus overlooking Macon's historic district hosts co-educational college preparatory classes for boys and girls.

Other noteworthy college prep schools include Stratford Academy, Tattnall Square Academy, and Windsor Academy. Several large capital improvement programs have begun at these schools as well, updating campuses and classrooms. Together, these schools enhance the Macon area's excellent educational standards.

STRONG COMMUNITY SUPPORT

Impressive community involvement underscores the educational system here. More than 14,000 volunteers shared their time and talents with public school students in the 1999-2000 school year alone. Educators work extensively with local businesses and the Greater Macon Chamber of Commerce to design appropriate classes for a highly trained workforce. Their group efforts also create mentoring, internships, and student employment opportunities through the Greater Middle Georgia Youth Apprenticeship program.

In 2000, Georgia's state government worked with BellSouth Corporation to initiate the nation's largest broadband infrastructure project ever—connecting all of Georgia. Every Bibb County classroom already has at least one computer, and soon every school statewide will have high-speed Internet access for expanded on-line capabilities. The Bibb County Public School System maintains contact with the community and students through a continually updated Web site and other outreach programs, such as 24-hour cable video programming.

The innovative Macon 2000 Partnership program begun in 1992 has served as a catalyst for much of the increased public awareness and community action benefiting Macon schools. The group helped to implement a variety of programs for students at little or no expense to taxpayers by leveraging local, state, and federal grants and resources. From structural improvements at Northeast High School to creating Youth Leadership Bibb County, the list of accomplishments truly reflects the community's commitment to its youth.

• More than 24,000 students attend classes at forty-one schools throughout the Macon County Public School System.
(top) Photo by Ken Krakow
(left) Photo by Leah Yetter

ACCESSIBLE EDUCATION BEYOND HIGH SCHOOL

Several post-secondary schools in the area help tend the city's vested interest in its future leaders. Two of these schools, Central Georgia Technical College and Macon State College, began as a result of Macon's economic growth in the late 1950s and early 1960s. Ironically, the educational link between employers and able workers was forged decades earlier by a Middle Georgian. State Senator and U.S. Congressman Dudley Mays Hughes introduced the historic Smith-Hughes Vocational Education Act of 1917, paving the way for federal funds for vocational institutions.

• (top) Wireless computer connection is available throughout Mount De Sales Academy's downtown campus. Photo by Beau Cabell

• (right) Macon residents understand that a quality education begins with community involvement and support for schools. Photo by Sherry DiBari

Today, the Central Georgia Technical College (CGTC), formerly Macon Technical Institute, works closely with local industry leaders to define applicable classroom studies. The school offers associate degrees, certificates and diplomas in high-demand areas such as health, aerospace, and business. CGTC also participates in Georgia's renowned QuickStart program, helping employers recruit, screen, and train a highly productive workforce—at no cost to the business.

With satellite campuses at Milledgeville and Eatonton, CGTC operates its main Macon campus just off Eisenhower Parkway. Comprised of eight contemporary buildings, the CGTC campus also hosts the Middle Georgia Police Academy. Notably, the Georgia Public Safety Training Center in nearby

Forsyth ranks as one of the world's most advanced facilities of its kind and complements the state's twenty-one training centers.

West of CGTC on Eisenhower Parkway lies Macon State College. This proactive school holds the same accreditation as CGTC and the two schools allow some cooperative study. Macon State College also serves as a scholastic gateway within the University System of Georgia. Like CGTC, Macon State College began in the 1960s in response to the local demand for highly trained graduates. The school opened as Macon Junior College in 1968, thanks to forward-thinking leaders and voters who supported establishment of a two-year institution.

As the 167-acre Macon Junior College campus sprouted more buildings over time, its mission grew, too. The name changed in 1997 to Macon State College, reflecting the addition of baccalaureate degrees in five majors. The school also added classes at Robins Air Force Base and in Warner Robins along the way. Known for its technology-based and health-professions programs, Macon State College remains an educational centerpiece of the community.

The University System of Georgia adds two more institutions to the area's educational roster. Georgia College & State University began in nearby Milledgeville as the Georgia State College for Women (novelist Flannery O'Connor's alma mater). Historic buildings grace the Milledgeville campus and underscore the school's prestigious stature. Georgia College & State University offers nursing, education, criminal justice, and business courses at its Macon campus.

A satellite campus in Macon for Fort Valley State University (FVSU) also expands the educational opportunities here. Established in 1895 as Fort Valley Normal and Industrial School and designated as a Land-Grant College for Negroes, the school became one of the first Negro colleges to receive full membership in the Southern Association of Colleges and Schools. Today, FVSU offers undergraduate and graduate courses in areas such as agriculture, home economics, and education. Its mission continues to reinforce its rigorous academic standards.

HISTORIC INSTITUTIONS GRACE THE CITY

Macon's educational palette features two of the South's most venerable private post-secondary schools. Both Wesleyan College and Mercer University continually rank among the top private institutions cited by *U.S. News and World Report's* annual school reviews. Equally rich in scholarly achievements and historic contributions, their invitingly pristine campuses grace Macon with well-conceived architecture.

Wesleyan College, established in 1836 as the first college in the world chartered to grant degrees to women, originally overlooked Macon from a formidable structure on the crest of College Street. The first college alumnae association formed here, as well as the first two Greek societies for women—now known as Alpha Delta Pi and Phi Mu. In 1928, the school moved to Macon's pastoral Rivoli area.

By the year 2000, Wesleyan completed its exhaustive renovation plan for every building on the sprawling 200-acre campus, plus construction of four new buildings. Cherokee Brick & Tile Company, a Macon firm, supplied the school with its own brick design for the landmark Georgian-style buildings. The massive construction project added some forty-seven miles of fiber-optic

• Art students from Westside High School share their spirit of creativity by painting a sports mural at Freedom Park Recreation Center. Photos by Woody Marshall

cable, providing greater networking capabilities for the highly computerized campus. Indeed, Wesleyan provides each full-time student with a computer to use for studies and to keep upon graduation. An affiliate of the United Methodist Church, Wesleyan enjoys a worldwide reputation for infusing technology and research into a strong liberal arts program covering twenty-four areas of study.

Mercer University also grew from a religious heritage and thrives today as one of the largest Baptist-affiliated institutions in the world. The school began in Penfield, Georgia, in 1833, and moved to Macon in 1871. Arching trees shade the ivy-laced campus in Macon and frame the picturesque architecture. Not all of these beautiful buildings are old, however. An energetic capital improvement campaign for Mercer's Macon and Atlanta campuses is bringing upgrades as well as new construction. Campus apartments and a new Greek Village already are completed, and plans call for a special events and athletics convocation center, a music building, classrooms, and a new student center.

With its dual campuses and statewide outreach programs, Mercer now counts nearly 7,000 students. They pursue degrees in liberal arts, business, engineering, education, medicine, pharmacy, law, and theology. In fact, Mercer offers more programs than any other independent institution of its size.

Because Mercer's graduates often remain in the Middle Georgia area, they have helped to actively support the school's role as a community partner. Mercer's Executive Forum, an eminent business enrichment program, sponsors appearances by nationally recognized leaders in business, the media, and government for Macon and Atlanta audiences. Mercer also remains committed to downtown Macon's redevelopment. Mercer's Office of University Advancement, the Macon Symphony Orchestra offices, and the School of Medicine facilities found "new" homes in renovated downtown buildings. As manager for the county-owned Grand Opera House, Mercer also contributes directly to the city's cultural exposure.

Countless educational opportunities exist through Macon's schools. Fortunately, more students can realize their educational goals now because of Georgia's HOPE (Helping Outstanding Pupils Educationally) program. Funded by the Georgia Lottery, HOPE provides scholarships for high school graduates to attend vocational schools, colleges, and universities. This incentive not only benefits area students, it also represents a worthwhile investment in Bibb County's next generation of leaders. ✻

• Central Georgia Technical College's eight-building campus is located off Eisenhower Boulevard. The school participates in the state's QuickStart program, which helps companies recruit, screen, and train employees. Photo by Ken Krakow

• Fort Valley State University, established in 1895, offers undergraduate and graduate courses in agriculture, home economics, and education. Photo by Ken Krakow

• (above and opposite) Macon State College, known for its technology-based and health-professions programs, is situated on a 167-acre campus. Photos by Ken Krakow

STUDENT LIFE CENTER

• (above) Picturesque architecture is a hallmark of Mercer University, a Macon institution since 1871. Photo by Ken Krakow

• (right) Students meet in front of Mercer's Administration Building in 1894. Photo courtesy of the Middle Georgia Archives

• (left) In 2000 historic Wesleyan College completed an extensive campus-wide renovation, plus construction of four new buildings.
Photo by Ken Krakow

• (below) In 1910 Wesleyan College was located in this formidable building on College Street. The school moved to its present campus in 1928.
Photo courtesy of the Middle Georgia Archives

CHAPTER SIX

6

Caring for Body & Spirit

Macon's forefathers sought to combine a healthy spirit and a healthy body. Their foresight laid the foundation for today's burgeoning religious community. The nationally recognized medical community here, which includes four hospitals, also traces its roots to the city's early days.

The presence of many historic churches adds to the city's charm. Photo by Ken Krakow

The first baptism on the continent reportedly took place here during Hernando DeSoto's 1540 explorations when his priests christened a native along the Ocmulgee's riverbanks. Perhaps this gave the city forefathers inspiration; by 1826 they organized Episcopal, Presbyterian, Methodist, and Baptist congregations in Macon. The Mulberry Methodist Church, established then, built the city's first house of worship in 1828 and still holds services on the same site.

Many of Macon's places of worship lend historic beauty to the city's skyline, and several of these landmarks trace their origins to the 1800s. The years following the Civil War solidified the role of organized religion throughout the South, as churches often provided the only feasible source of socializing in rural communities. Religion for all denominations continues to hold a prominent place in Macon's culture, blending strong values, clear standards, and community pride with lessons of faith.

HEEDING THE DOCTOR'S ADVICE

One of Macon's early leaders and its first physician, Dr. Ambrose Baber, advised the fledgling city in 1826 to set aside wooded land below Seventh Street to benefit the community's health. History books note that crowds congregated in the "city reserve" before the Civil War. However, construction for Central City Park on the reserved property waited until 1870 when Macon prepared to host the next year's State Fair. Sporting one of the world's best horse-racing facilities, the park probably wasn't exactly what Dr. Baber envisioned. Nevertheless, his adopted city proved itself a healthy place to live compared to many other Southern towns stricken with yellow fever and cholera; historic documents show no cases originating here.

**• (top) Christ Episcopal Church, built in 1851, is located downtown on Walnut Street.
Photo by Beau Cabell**

**• (right) A men's group from New Hope Baptist Church assembled for this photograph in the 1940s.
Photo courtesy of the Middle Georgia Archives**

Macon's early physicians, dentists, and apothecaries cared for patients without a city hospital until 1895. In that year the King's Daughters, a group of concerned women, purchased a brick residence on Pine Street for the Macon Hospital Association. Renovations created four private rooms and sixteen ward beds. The first ambulance run took place in 1900, charting the hospital's course as an emergency center. The next year brought the Training School for Nurses, also prophetic for the facility's eventual role as a teaching hospital.

The city took over Macon Hospital in 1915. A reorganization in 1968 formed the Macon-Bibb County Hospital Authority. Three years later the facility's name changed to the Medical Center of Central Georgia, reflecting its expanded capabilities and regional outreach.

A NETWORK OF MEDICAL SERVICES

Today's Medical Center of Central Georgia, part of the Central Georgia Health System, blends advanced medical technology and treatments with time-proven notions of comfort and care. Still located downtown near its original site, the Medical Center of Central Georgia has become a 518-bed acute-care, regional medical center and teaching hospital. The hospital admits more than 150,000 patients annually without regard to race, religion, or ability to pay. Indigent care costs reach well into the millions of dollars every year. In 1994 the Medical Center of Central Georgia earned recognition as one of the top 100 hospitals in the United States.

An extensive network of more than twenty-five subspecialty centers complements the main hospital facility and allows the Medical Center to tailor its care for patients. The Children's Hospital at the Medical Center tends to ill youngsters amid toys, books, and colorfully decorated rooms. Similarly, the Family Birth Center welcomes expectant mothers with twenty-two private suites, each with thoughtful touches like massage tubs and sleeper sofas for fathers.

• St. Joseph's Catholic Church is an architectural treasure both inside and out. The church's twin spires rise 200 feet and are a familiar sight on Macon's skyline. Photos by Ken Krakow

• During the 20th century, the scope of health care changed dramatically in Macon. Above, patients in the 1930s received care at Macon Hospital on Pine Street. The facility opened in 1895 as Bibb County's first hospital. Below, doctors at St. Luke's Hospital perform surgery in 1950.
Photos courtesy of the Middle Georgia Archives

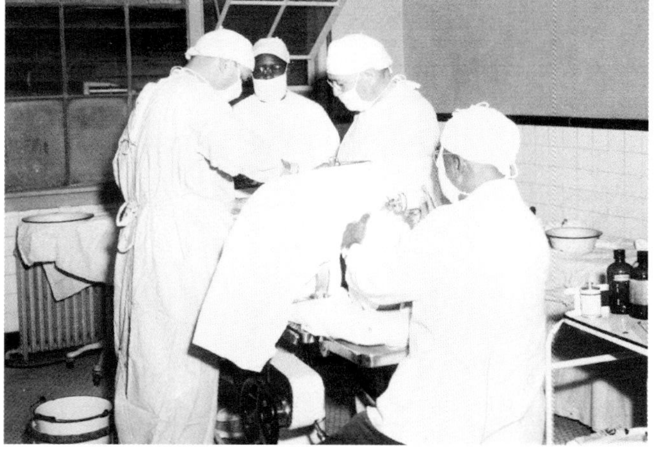

Other specialty facilities include the Children's Health Center, the Family Health Center, Focal Pointe Women, the Pavilion for inpatient psychiatric care, the Cancer Life Center, Hospice of Central Georgia, the Diabetes Treatment Center, the Georgia Heart Center, and the Surgery Center. Five conveniently located urgent-care centers treat minor illnesses and injuries seven days a week.

The Emergency Center, the only one with 24-hour trauma surgery capabilities in Central Georgia, responds to some 28,000 emergency calls from Bibb, Twiggs, and Jones counties every year. In 2000, the Medical Center assisted Jones County in securing funds for an ambulance station in downtown Gray. Cooperative community projects such as this reflect the hospital's broad mission.

The Medical Center defines itself as an integral part of the community and derives its strength from the community as well. This reciprocal support fortifies various outreach efforts, too, such as the Neighborhood Healthcare Centers, Golden Opportunities-Seniors Helping Seniors groups, and educational services for topics ranging from baby care to weight loss. The Medical Center also emphasizes education for its staff and ranks as one of the country's top 20 teaching hospitals. Nearby Mercer University sends many of its medical students to learn from the experienced hands at the Medical Center, and graduates often stay with the hospital. Now more than 3,000 physicians, nurses, technicians, and other personnel make the Medical Center of Central Georgia the county's largest employer—enhancing the community's economic health, too.

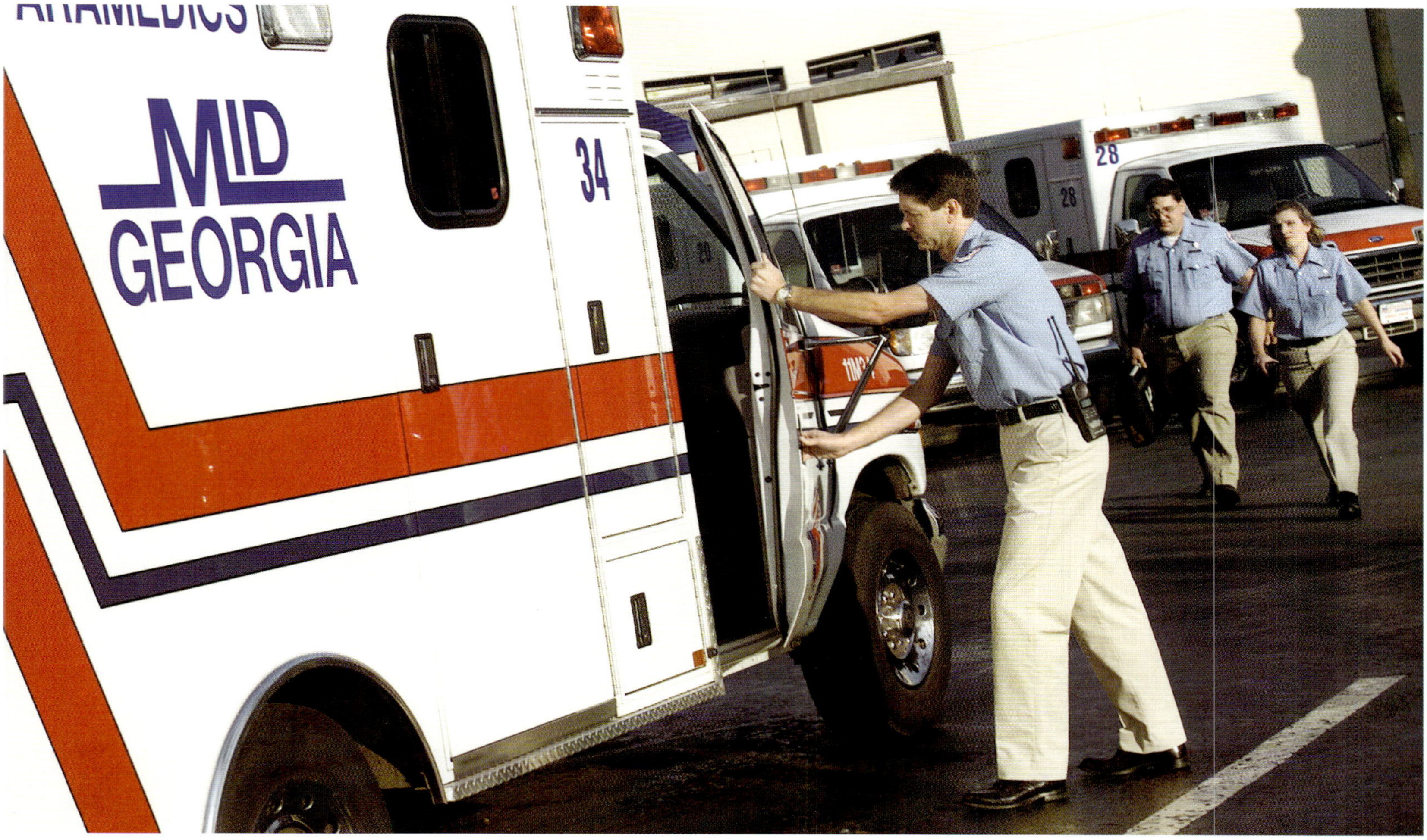

• (above) When seconds are critical, Macon's medical workers quickly provide state-of-the-art care.

• (left) Modern facilities throughout the city meet a wide range of medical needs.
Photos by Ken Krakow

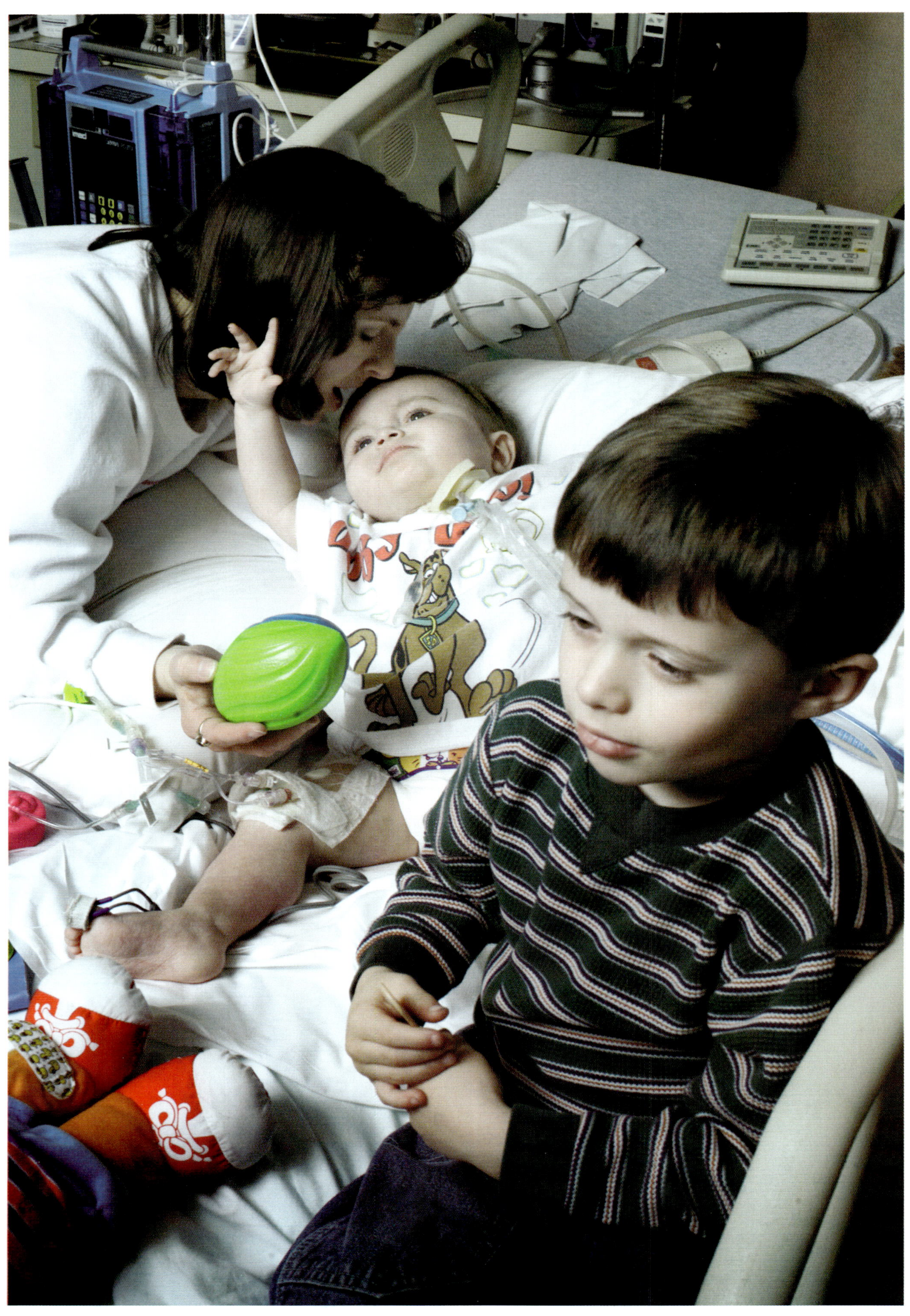

• Children's Hospital offers specialized care to youngsters from infancy through age 16. Photo by Ken Krakow

EXPANDED CARE COVERAGE

Macon's health-care options expanded dramatically in 1971 when Hospital Corporation of America (HCA) opened a hospital here. Today, Coliseum Medical Centers ranks among the country's top hospitals, consistently implementing the latest equipment and procedures. Its 258-bed full-service hospital employs about 1,000 personnel, including 115 physicians; services range from cardiac catheterization and 24-hour emergency care to speech therapy and respiratory care.

Drawing patients from the entire Middle Georgia region, Coliseum Health System incorporates sophisticated technology and treatment within specific divisions, including The Breast Health Center, Same Day Surgery Center, Women's Center, Coliseum Psychiatric Center, Industrial Medicine Center, Metabolic Center, Wound Healing Center, and Rehabilitation Center. A border of brilliant crepe myrtles surrounds several of these centers, plus four physician office buildings, on a park-like hillside overlooking the Ocmulgee River.

Coliseum Medical Centers further increased its accessibility through mergers in 1998 with Middle Georgia Hospital and Macon Northside Hospital. Opened in 1911 as Macon's first privately owned hospital, Middle Georgia Hospital now offers inpatient and outpatient medical-surgical care at its 119-bed facility. Macon Northside Hospital, which began in 1984 as part of the Charter Medical Corporation, now features one of the area's most charming and technically advanced family birth centers. The 103-bed medical-surgical hospital offers emergency care as well as inpatient and outpatient services.

WELLNESS WITHOUT BOUNDARIES

Macon's large and diverse health-care community receives considerable support from related businesses and organizations, such as home health care and specialized therapeutic and medical centers. The Macon-Bibb County Health Department promotes healthful living through immunizations, classes, and other community-based programs. The Wellness Center-Macon Health Club, affiliated with the Medical Center of Central Georgia, encourages people of all ages to enjoy active lifestyles. Several other local workout centers also keep Maconites in shape. Whether it's walking at the Colonial Mall Macon or playing tennis, mountain-bike riding or golfing, swimming or rowing, endless opportunities for fun and fitness attract a regular following in Macon. ❋

• Macon's newest residents are ensured of the finest treatment, and they benefit from the latest medical technology. Photo by Ken Krakow

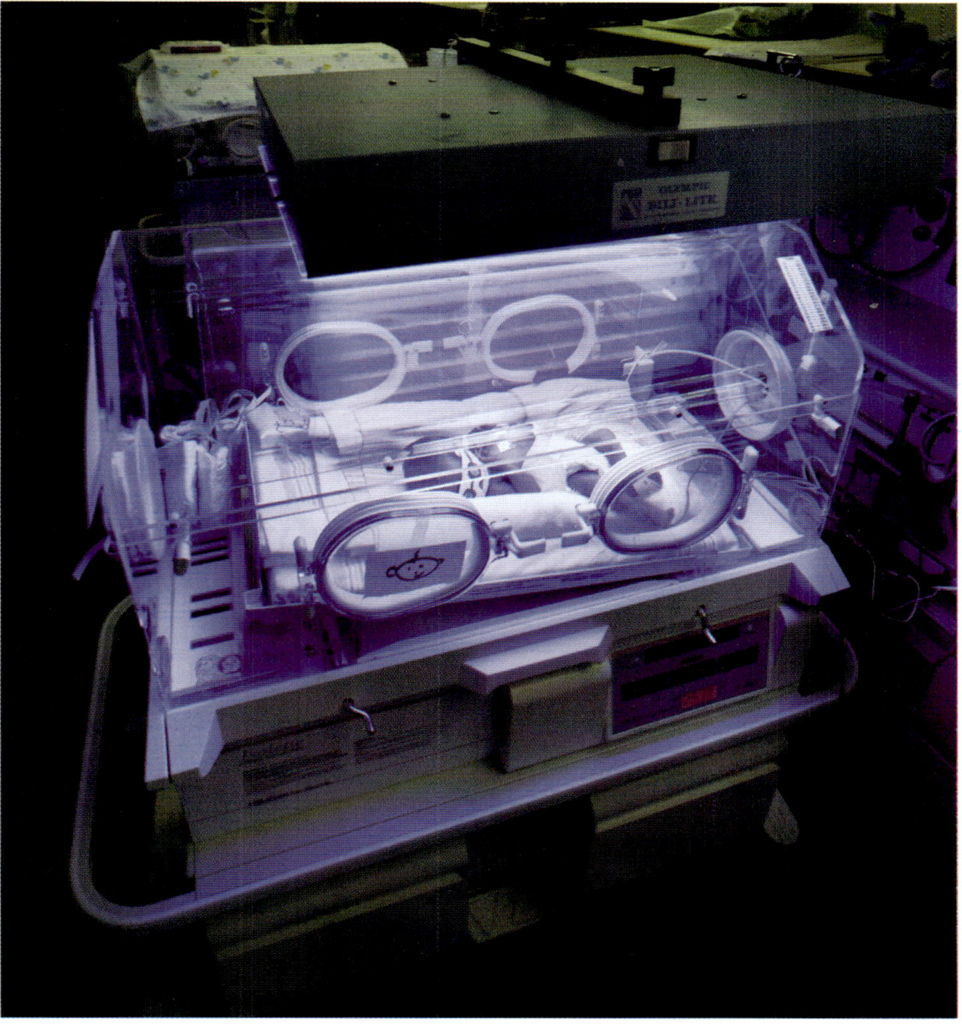

ZAXBY'S
THE CLUBHOUSE

CHAPTER SEVEN

7

Endless Happenings

Spectators cheer exuberantly for their favorite teams at area venues, adding a spirited hometown advantage for the baseball, hockey, and football players. From fishing to golf and from theater performances to music concerts, Maconites always find plenty to see and do any time of year.

The Macon Whoopees have received a warm welcome from fans since the minor-league team returned to town in 1996. Photo by Ken Krakow

• Through the years, many baseball greats have appeared at Luther Williams Field. Top, Pete Rose slides to third base in 1962, when he played for the Macon Peaches. Below, in 1956 Hank Aaron and his fellow Milwaukee Braves squared off against the Macon Peaches. Aaron is shown strolling across home plate after hitting a home run.
Photos courtesy of the Middle Georgia Archives

Horse-drawn carriages delivered spectators to Macon's venues long before the first paved roads. Audiences came to see everything from thrilling horse races to elaborate stage productions. The all-American pastime of baseball ranked among the favored sporting events, and the New York Yankees played here as early as 1917.

Luther Williams Field, built in 1929 and refurbished in 1992, hosted home teams such as the Macon Peaches, part of the South Atlantic League. Now the country's second oldest minor league baseball park, Luther Williams Field still grooms young players for major league teams. The Macon Braves Single A team has sent many successful prospects to the Atlanta Braves over the years.

Macon's proximity to Atlanta has fueled support for other home teams, too. In 1973, local interest in the Atlanta Flames hockey team helped spur the minor-league Macon Whoopees. The team played only through 1974. Reintroduced with the same name in 1996, the renewed Macon Whoopees quickly gained fans and even earned a play-off spot in the 1999-2000 season.

Macon's tremendous sports enthusiasm welcomed the Georgia Sports Hall of Fame when it opened in the city's downtown museum district in 1999. This 43,000-square-foot facility pays an exciting tribute to the state's top high school, collegiate, professional, and amateur athletes. Legendary players Henry "Hank" Aaron and Fran Tarkenton are among inductees to the Hall of Fame.

MORE THAN SPECTATORS HERE

Macon's abundance of sunny days encourages an array of outdoor activities, especially sports. The Macon-Bibb County Parks and Recreation Department organizes a full schedule of programs for basketball, softball, swimming, soccer, and tennis. The John Drew Smith Tennis Center, recognized as one of the country's top twenty-five public tennis facilities, hosts several of the Parks and Rec-sponsored competitions during the year. Public and private schools train football, baseball, basketball, and soccer players, as well as swimmers, runners, and other young athletes.

Golfers at all skill levels make the most of the temperate climate, too. Public and private courses wind through the hilly Middle Georgia terrain, while numerous driving ranges allow time to hone swings. Towering above I-75, the Ironwoods' gigantic driving range screen beckons golfers and draws curious looks from passersby.

Prevailing blue skies also entice area anglers and boaters to nearby Lake Tobesofkee. This man-made recreational area, completed in 1969, features sandy beaches, playgrounds, picnic areas, tennis courts, and campgrounds along its 35-mile shoreline. Locals mark their calendars for the last weekend in October, when Arrowhead Park at Lake Tobesofkee hosts a spectacular arts and crafts festival beneath an awning of autumn-hued leaves.

Several more wooded parks, lakes, and nature preserves surrounding Macon also invite exploration. Northward, the rushing waters and rocky outcrops in High Falls State Park attract photographers with stunning scenes. And the quiet pools and reedy marshes to the south in the 6,000-acre Bond Swamp National Wildlife Refuge also promise memorable imagery.

Overlooking the Bond Swamp, a unique preserve called Brown's Mount rewards naturalists with wildlife encounters—perhaps even glimpses of soaring bald eagles. Macon's Museum of Arts and Sciences directs the special environmental study and appreciation programs for Brown's Mount. Day treks and astronomy-embellished night hikes remain among the most popular activities.

Less intrepid stargazers regularly scope the night skies from the Mark Smith Planetarium at the Museum of Arts and Sciences. Daytime visitors explore the museum's fascinating interactive exhibits and galleries indoors or wander outdoors to the Back Yard to see the museum's live collections in forest, aquatic, and desert habitats. The 14-acre shaded campus also features the historic cabin of Macon writer Harry Stillwell Edwards, as well as a caboose, picnic areas, and nature trails.

FOUR SEASONS OF ENTERTAINMENT

Balancing sports and outdoor activities, the city's vast cultural arts events, performances, exhibitions, and classes round out the calendar. Creative energy builds with MidSummer Macon, a cultural arts learning and performing extravaganza on the Wesleyan College campus. Writers, dancers, musicians, actors, and other artists enliven this annual event with guidance from visiting artists and several arts groups, including the Macon Arts Alliance.

The Macon Arts Alliance, now located in the Boulevard Art Gallery downtown, nurtures the diverse art community here. This non-profit organization advocates arts programs in education and actively coordinates funding for the arts. Macon Arts Alliance also sponsors First Night Macon, a family-oriented New Year's Eve celebration, and the Georgia Music Festival in September.

Macon's local theaters, also involved with the Macon Arts Alliance, enhance the performing arts options here. The longstanding Macon Little Theater tends to stage more traditional and popular plays; conversely, Theatre Macon leans toward contemporary work. Staging performances in the renovated Ritz Movie House downtown, Theatre Macon takes pride in its intimate setting. Other top-notch theatrical offerings include productions at Mercer University, Wesleyan College, and Macon State College. And, Forsyth's Backlot Players, Community Children's Theatre, and Warner Robins Little Theatre also add to the busy box-office season here.

Perhaps most often in the limelight because of its rich history, the gloriously restored Grand Opera House regularly draws large audiences in Macon. The ornate building opened

• (above) The Macon Braves make their home at Luther Williams Field, the country's second oldest minor league baseball park. Photo by Thomas Metthe

• (left) The Georgia Sports Hall of Fame pays tribute to the state's most influential athletes, including Hank Aaron and Fran Tarkenton. Photo by Ken Krakow

• (top right) Theatre Macon has earned recognition as one of the state's best community theaters by the Georgia Council for the Arts.
Photo by Leah Yetter

• (top left) The Academy of Music opened in 1884 in an ornate building on Mulberry Street. Right, by 1908 the structure had become the Grand Opera House. Today the Grand Opera House is fully restored and serves as a performing arts center for Mercer University.
Photos courtesy of the Middle Georgia Archives

in 1884 as the Academy of Music. Since then, its massive stage has featured performances as varied as death scenes by actress Sarah Bernhardt, vaudeville acts by comedians George Burns and Gracie Allen, and acoustic solos by pianist George Winston. Now on the National Register of Historic Places, the Grand Opera House returned to its educational heritage in the late 1990s as a performing arts center for Mercer University. Its calendar boasts a full season of Broadway shows each year, as well as performances by the Macon Symphony Orchestra.

Occasionally, the Grand Opera House also features dance productions, such as the exciting modern dance of the Macon Moving Company Dance Theatre. Formed in 1993, this semi-professional troupe often collaborates with the Imani Ensemble, a teen dance company specializing in African dance, mime, and modern dance. Ballet continues to enchant audiences, too. The Nutcracker of Middle Georgia's annual production, also staged at the Grand Opera House, has become a holiday tradition. Youngsters inspired by the graceful dancers can find instruction through one of many local dance schools.

A LEGENDARY MUSICAL HERITAGE

The Douglass Theatre, a venue counterpart to the Grand Opera House, opened in 1921 for the city's black audiences. African-American entrepreneur Charles H. Douglass built this distinctive movie theater and vaudeville hall, showcasing the film work of early 20th century blacks. Early jazz and blues stars, such as Bessie Smith and Ma Rainey, appeared there, as did Cab Calloway and Duke Ellington. By the 1960s, several musical greats started their rise to fame at the Douglass Theatre. Maconites Little Richard, Otis Redding, and James Brown, among other black musicians, tasted stardom for the first time from the Douglass Theatre stage.

Otis Redding's manager, Phil Walden, expanded his role in American music history when he founded Capricorn Recording Studios. Capricorn cultivated the new "Southern Rock" sound, and the studio signed the 1970s hit band the Allman Brothers, among other popular groups. When two Allman Brothers band members, Duane Allman and Berry Oakley, both died in tragic accidents near the band's Vineville Avenue "Big House," Macon received unprecedented media attention. Their final resting places in Rose Hill Cemetery still bring faithful fans from around the world.

While popular music put Macon on the rock-and-roll map, other musical styles earned local performers well-deserved international acclaim, too. Allan Evans gained fame as an opera singer. Violinist Robert McDuffie travels the globe to perform with some of the world's finest symphonies today. He returns to Macon periodically for hometown appearances.

Since forming in 1975, the Macon Civic Chorale has performed two local concerts each year. The group's lilting voices have carried them all the way to New York's Carnegie Hall and even as far as Europe. The Georgian Renaissance Singers, Jazz Association of Macon, Macon Concert Association, Macon Youth Symphony, Middle Georgia Barbershop Quartet, Sweet Adelines, and Wings of Harmony Chorus also regularly share their musical talents with appreciative audiences in Macon and elsewhere.

From genteel requiems to toe-tapping country tunes, the musical variety in Macon offers all music fans a hearty sampling during the year. Indeed, a variety of cultural and recreational venues gives Maconites a world of entertaining options. ❋

• (top) Many musical greats got their start at the Douglass Theatre, shown in 1940. Otis Redding, left, made his stage debut at the Douglass in the early 1960s. Photos courtesy of the Middle Georgia Archives

• (far left) After an extensive renovation, the Douglass Theatre once again is an entertainment showcase.
Photo by Woody Marshall

• Whether Macon residents are looking for spirited competition or plain relaxation, the area offers ideal spots for any recreational activity. Photos by Woody Marshall

• (top) Photo by Ken Krakow

• (left) Photo by Robert Seay

CHAPTER EIGHT

8

Central Georgia's Showcase

Macon's expanding collection of museums and attractions showcases the area's rich history, extraordinary musical heritage, and cultural diversity. Exciting events throughout the year complement the mix, creating treasured memories for visitors and Maconites alike.

Every October the Georgia State Fair entertains Macon residents with exciting rides, informative exhibits, and fantastic food. Photo by Ken Krakow

Surrounded by a landscape white with cotton, 19th-century Macon society waltzed through a procession of brightly colored diversions every year. Lavish in-town entertaining required suitable homes, often with ballrooms for dancing or musical performances. Among the city's most prestigious addresses, the magnificent antebellum Hay House still stands as a tribute to architectural ingenuity, prosperity, and Southern hospitality.

William Butler Johnston and his wife, Anne, built Hay House between 1855 and 1859 in the splendid Italian Renaissance Revival style. Its 18,000 square feet incorporated the era's latest technologies, such as indoor bathrooms, hot and cold running water, speaker tube "intercom" system, and central heating. The house even burned gaslights before the White House in Washington, D.C. Now a National Historic Landmark under the ownership of the Georgia Trust for Historic Preservation, "The Palace of the South" is available for guided tours and private rentals.

• Hay House was built by entrepreneur William B. Johnston, and construction was completed in 1859. The home, which earned the name "Palace of the South," is open for tours. Photo by Ken Krakow

Several neighboring historic homes welcome tourists, too. The Cannonball House and Confederate Museum, built in the 1850s, gained local fame as Macon's only home damaged during the Civil War. Sidney Lanier Cottage, dating to 1840, also features guided tours. This modest structure is the birthplace of renowned poet and musician Sidney Lanier and now houses the Middle Georgia Historical Society headquarters. Nearby on Coleman Hill, Mercer University offers appointment-only tours of Woodruff House, a Greek Revival mansion built in 1836.

Many more stunning homes peer from behind sentinel magnolias and live oaks along city streets. Macon reportedly has more acreage listed on the National Register of Historic Places than any other city in the South. Some homes have become restaurants and businesses, such as the 1842 Inn, an elegant bed-and-breakfast converted from a stately Greek Revival residence. A 1910 English-style home designed by esteemed Georgia architect Neel Reid provides a picturesque setting for banquets, receptions, and meetings. Called the Garden Club Center, this lovely home also is headquarters for the Federated Garden Clubs of Macon.

Most other historic homes in Macon remain private residences, including the distinctive Raines-Carmichael House. Shaped like a modified Greek cross, this hilltop home has earned National Historic Landmark designation for its compelling design.

Any night of the year, evening strollers can enjoy the dramatic illumination of more than thirty historic residences. Professionally designed, the "Lights On Macon" tour presents a unique, self-guided glimpse of the past. The Macon-Bibb County Convention and Visitors Bureau developed a variety of self-guided walking tours for daytime, too. Similarly, the Rose Hill Ramble presents a fascinating tour through the city's historic hillside cemetery, recalling some of Macon's most famous names.

For those who prefer more restful sightseeing excursions, Sidney's Tours provides guided tours aboard an air-conditioned bus, and a new trolley tour also offers insights to the city's past.

• Hay House featured some technological marvels for the 1800s, including central heating for its 18,000 square feet. The Italianate mansion now is a National Historic Landmark.
Photo courtesy of the Middle Georgia Archives

HONORING ACHIEVEMENT

Today, most tourists here visit at least one of the area's many museums. In the downtown museum district, three fascinating facilities honor the state's most revered athletes, musicians, artists, and visionaries, many of whom called Macon home. Across the street from the exciting Georgia Sports Hall of Fame, the Georgia Music Hall of Fame celebrates various musical styles along the streets of its lively "Tune Town." Macon's own musicians, Otis Redding, the Allman Brothers Band, and Little Richard have been inducted already, joining hundreds of talented Georgians.

The tribute to outstanding artistry continues just a few steps away at the Tubman African American Museum. Consistently ranked as one of the top 10 visual arts institutions in the state by the Georgia Council for the Arts, the Tubman African American Museum focuses on the art, history, and culture of blacks. One of the museum's fourteen galleries features Wilfred Stroud's panoramic mural depicting the African journey from early slavery to contemporary leadership. Another popular gallery honors black military leaders and showcases the Medal of Honor awarded to Maconite Sergeant Rodney Davis, who gave his life to save fellow soldiers during the Vietnam War. The largest facility of its kind in Georgia, the Tubman African American Museum also offers children's cultural arts classes and sponsors various performances and events, including the Pan-African Festival.

A museum inside the nearby Douglass Theatre similarly showcases the contribution of black entertainers and entrepreneurs. Examples

• History buffs will enjoy a long walk through Rose Hill Cemetery, which dates back to 1840. Duane Allman of the Allman Brothers Band and fellow band member Berry Oakley are buried at Rose Hill. Photo by Ken Krakow

of Macon's exceptional black heritage surround the city as well. Pleasant Hill Historic District, one of the first historically black neighborhoods on the National Register of Historic Places, embraces Linwood Cemetery, where some 4,000 black residents were laid to rest. The Booker T. Washington Community Center, also located in Pleasant Hill, and the Ruth Hartley Mosely Memorial Women's Center honor native visionaries who saw a future without color boundaries. In Central City Park, the Benny Scott Plaza recognizes one of the South's first black engineers and a dedicated community volunteer.

A PAST PRESERVED FOR THE FUTURE

African-American soldiers, particularly Air Force pilots, received recognition when the Museum of Aviation Flight and Technology Center at Robins Air Force Base in Warner Robins opened its popular exhibit, "America's Black Eagles—Tuskegee Pioneers and Beyond" in 1997. This 5,000-square-foot presentation of African-American pilots' World War II memorabilia features the BT-13 basic trainer aircraft, bringing the total number of aircraft and missile displays to 93. One of the nation's largest aerospace museums, this education and federal historic preservation center sprawls across 43 acres with indoor and outdoor exhibits.

The Museum of Aviation's extensive display of Georgia's Native American artifacts, paintings, and historical documents surprises many visitors, since it seems incongruous with flight. History and the land, rather than the sky, connects Robins Air Force Base to Native Americans. In 1992, researchers discovered an archaeological

treasure trove of more than 30 pristine sites within the Robins Air Force Base acreage. Members of the Muscogee (Creek) Nation, whose ancestors once gathered on these lands, assisted with the exhibit, lending authentic interpretation to the story of Native Americans who lived in the area from 8,000 B.C. to A.D. 1837.

Tracing a path through history often requires a different sort of tour guide, and the experts at Washington Memorial Library and Middle Georgia Archives have become world-famous for their abilities. The Genealogical & Historical Room holds more than 16,000 volumes and 6,000 micro-film reels covering early pioneers and Revolutionary War veterans. Among its many resources, the library also houses an African-American collection, issues of *The Macon Telegraph* dating to 1823, materials for the blind and, of course, hundreds of thousands of books for adults and children.

• The Tubman African American Museum is one of Macon's top tourist attractions, with more than 65,000 visitors a year.
(top) Photo by Woody Marshall
(below) Photo Ken Krakow

THE CELEBRATION CONTINUES

Just as many early Maconites reveled in their party season, today's residents look forward to grand celebrations throughout the year. The annual Cherry Blossom Festival in March, named a Top 100 Event in North America, promises 10 days of entertainment, food, and fun—more than 500 events in all. Some 236,000 Yoshino cherry trees in Macon, far more than Washington, D.C., form a princess-pink canopy to herald spring's return. Warm weather also brings the annual Pan-African Festival of Georgia and the charming Secret Gardens Tour, a benefit event that allows flower enthusiasts to wander through some of the city's most enchanting backyards.

• (left) The state's musical history comes to life at the Georgia Music Hall of Fame. The museum contains a treasure trove of memorabilia and many interactive exhibits.

• (below) Tune Town, part of the Georgia Music Hall of Fame, is a village where every building pays tribute to a different genre of music. Audio is a large part of the Tune Town experience, and CD stations are common throughout the village.
Photos by Ken Krakow

• Throughout Macon, restaurants offer a wide range of fine fare and dining atmospheres. Photo by Ken Krakow

The cooler days of autumn usher in a full calendar of events, too. Maconites and visitors alike look forward to the Ocmulgee Indian Celebration, Georgia State Fair, and the Arrowhead Arts and Crafts Festival. The Sweet Georgia Jam in September also attracts a loyal following, as Macon celebrates Georgia's exceptional musical legacy.

Then it's not long before Macon's White Columns & Holly celebration rings in the holidays with performances, home tours, and festive lighting. Ranked as a Top 20 Event in the Southeast, White Columns & Holly sets a festive mood for the season. Kwanzaa tributes to African heritage enliven December days, too. On December 31, the First Night Macon celebration welcomes the New Year with family-oriented events that culminate in a magical fireworks display over the city. Macon's modern-day celebrations offer proof that the city remains as spirited and colorful as ever. ❋

• (left) Macon is home to many different cultural experiences. Japanese students perform at Coleman Hill during opening ceremonies for the Cherry Blossom Festival. Photo by Sherry DiBari

• (below) The Museum of Arts and Sciences features four galleries where artistic exhibits are rotated. Photo by Ken Krakow

• Visitors can explore the rich history of the area's Native American tribes at the Ocmulgee Indian Celebration. The annual event is held at the Ocmulgee National Monument.
Photos by Sherry DiBari

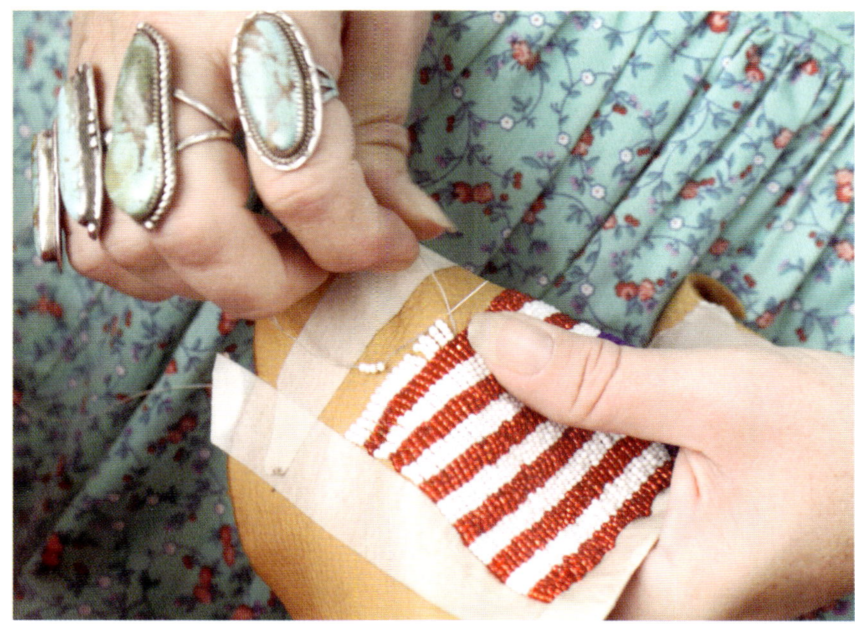

• (top) Photo by Sherry DiBari

• (right) Photo by Woody Marshall

With more than 200,000 cherry trees, Macon is the perfect home for the International Cherry Blossom Festival, held every March. The ten-day festival features hundreds of events, including concerts, historic tours, international cuisine, and multicultural exhibits.

• Photos by Woody Marshall

CHAPTER NINE

9

Forging A New History

With the new millennium comes an enhanced commitment to Macon's quality of life, economic strength, and cultural diversity. Plans forged today will stand as the framework for tomorrow's continued success.

Macon's revitalized downtown area beckons visitors with a variety of attractions, including the Georgia Music Hall of Fame's scenic fountains. Photo by Ken Krakow

Macon's forefathers envisioned a prosperous future for their river town. In those frontier days, perhaps nothing signified civility, stability, and commitment more than churches. By 1826, Episcopalian, Presbyterian, Methodist, and Baptist congregations formed here for both whites and blacks. The Mulberry Methodist Church built the city's first house of worship in 1828 and still holds services on the same site now. Macon's oldest church, the Christ Episcopal Church, hosted the marriage of famed poet Sidney Lanier. The oldest black Presbyterian church in Georgia originated here in 1838. Today, Macon's places of worship crown the city skyline, welcoming the faithful and encouraging community involvement.

Complementing the remarkably strong religious presence here, organizations of all types share a spirit of giving with the community. Some focus on assisting the economically disadvantaged. Others provide resources and support for those stricken with disabling diseases. Several groups work to build confidence and skills among the city's youth, and still others encourage networking and community involvement for area professionals. Volunteer Macon, a clearinghouse for all of the local non-profit organizations, helps match able hands to various tasks.

• (top) Coleman Hill offers a panoramic view of downtown Macon.

• (right) The city's older neighborhoods exude a quaint atmosphere and give residents the convenience of city living. Photos by Ken Krakow

A PLACE TO CALL HOME

The glorious homes along downtown streets exude a historic charm many people find irresistible. For those who prefer more contemporary styling, Macon's homebuilders and designers present an astounding variety of options. Many new homes nestle beside golf courses, waterways and stately pine forests. New subdivisions skirt both the northern and southern tiers of the city, too. Residential construction contracts zoomed upward 49 percent between 1999 and 2000, and the outlook remains promising for Bibb, Houston, Jones, Peach, and Twiggs counties.

In fact, the city's metropolitan statistical area (MSA) has steadily gained residents in recent years. By 1997, the population reached 316,230. Per capita personal income of $21,770 reported for that year also followed a trend of annual increases, according to the Bureau of Economic Analysis for the U.S. Department of Commerce.

Local economic forecasts remain positive, too. Macon's close ties to area colleges and universities encourage business innovations, a well-trained workforce, and greater employment opportunities. In 2000, the University System of Georgia's Intellectual Capital Partnership Program began a health information management program through Macon State College with hands-on training at Core Management Resources Group. By adding 200 jobs downtown, the venture promotes economic growth for the city.

As Macon expands, so does the need for well-prepared police, firefighters, and other emergency response personnel. Macon's professionals work diligently to preserve the fine quality of life here. Ongoing rigorous training refines their skills and hones their response times, actually helping to lower insurance costs for residents. Together, the city's affordable housing, strong employment opportunities, and exemplary safety systems bode well for Macon's future.

BUILDING ON SUCCESS

The framework for Macon's future takes shape in plans approved by today's civic leaders. Many exciting projects are benefitting both old and young, residents and visitors alike. The Ronald McDonald House will offer a quiet haven for out-of-town families with children hospitalized here. A new home for Macon's Boy Scouts and Girl Scouts opened recently and has expanded the capabilities of these popular organizations.

• (top) The citizens of Macon have made downtown a great place to work and play.
Photo by Woody Marshall

• (left) Macon's well-trained workforce and exemplary quality of life are attracting a growing number of companies.
Photo by Ken Krakow

Part of the growing downtown museum district, the new Tubman African American Museum will provide a spacious, contemporary facility for interactive exhibits, displays, discussions, and performances. Similarly, the prospect of a Children's Museum in downtown Macon—the only one of its kind in the state—has intrigued parents and youngsters alike. Cheerfully colored windowpanes enliven the historic five-story building downtown and hint at the excitement to come.

Other new construction will fortify Macon's bustling economy, such as expansion projects along the Eisenhower Parkway retail corridor. Eisenhower Crossing, a retail complex covering more than 500,000 square feet, will feature a collection of national stores as well as a neighborhood grocery.

Old favorites, such as Nu-Way Wieners, seize new opportunities today, too. First opened in 1916, Nu-Way still serves its private-label wieners smothered in secret-recipe chili sauce from the original diner on Cotton Avenue. The famous eatery began expanding with stores in the outlying areas in the 1990s. Nu-Way has plenty of company in the suburbs, of course, with more to come. Office buildings will sprout there, especially along Arkwright Road and other busy streets. New schools will also follow the influx of residents.

The Bibb County Public School System made provisions for future construction in the early 1990s, and upgrades to current schools abound already. The area's private schools similarly expect increased enrollment. In 2000, Stratford Academy opened a new 17,500-square-foot library, and the school intends to pursue additional campus enhancements. Likewise, Wesleyan College and Mercer University entered the new millennium with ambitious campus improvements and capital campaigns.

Not all plans on the drawing table call for entirely new construction. Many property owners choose to rebuild the interior of old buildings, leaving the exterior façade for the historic beauty. Clisby Elementary school along Vineville Avenue showcases the school's original architecture outside and incorporates the newest structural designs inside. Similarly, plans for the classic red brick

• The renovated Whittle School, shown below in 1908, serves a new function as office headquarters.
(top) Photo by Ken Krakow
(right) Photo courtesy of the Middle Georgia Archives

Lanier High School call for keeping the 1916 exterior while rebuilding the interior to house the Medical Center of Central Georgia's physician offices. Although not preservation in the truest sense, the technique offers a compromise that saves resources and lowers costs as it maintains historic ambiance.

Macon's revitalizing projects, such as those promoted by NewTown Macon, include more than brick-and-mortar structures. A proposed Ocmulgee Heritage Greenway extending along the river from Warner Robins to Juliette would create landscaped pathways, nature trails, and scenic parks along the Ocmulgee River. The peaceful Gateway Park, with its bubbling fountain at the corner of Martin Luther King Jr. Boulevard and Riverside Drive, will serve as the project's centerpiece.

Progress continues to pulse through Macon as strongly today as ever, echoing the resilient heartbeat of the South. Undoubtedly, Macon's future will continue to unfold like a grand magnolia blossom—lush, fresh, and ever appreciative of deep Southern roots. ❋

• (top) Scouting is one way Macon's young people meet with their friends and serve the community. Boy Scout troops meet in a newly constructed building on Confederate Way.

• (below) Girl Scouts show their creative flair while completing a craft project. Photos by Ken Krakow

• Macon has embarked on a development project to beautify the city's riverfront area. Photo by Ken Krakow

• (right) With dozens of quality hotels, Macon caters to both business travelers and tourists.

• (below) Herbert Smart Airport serves smaller aircraft, including private and corporate jets. Commercial flights are based at Middle Georgia Regional Airport. Photos by Ken Krakow

• (top) Dedicated public servants train diligently to serve the citizens of Macon.

• (left) A new water treatment facility enhances Macon's highly reliable system of utilities.
Photos by Ken Krakow

• The Children's Museum, a new addition to downtown, is filled with interactive exhibits that are fun and educational. Photo by Ken Krakow

• Historic Native American sites and high-tech enterprises are only two of the Macon area's many facets. Photos by Ken Krakow

• The city of Macon sparkles with manmade beauty and natural wonders.
Photos by Woody Marshall

• (top) Photo by Woody Marshall

• (right) Photo by Beau Cabell

Throughout the year, residents and visitors alike can enjoy the area's rich history, avenues to adventure, and Southern charm.

• Photos by Woody Marshall

PART TWO

CHAPTER TEN

10

Business, Finance, & the Professions

Photo by Ken Krakow

IKON OFFICE SOLUTIONS

IKON BUSINESS SERVICES

IKON Office Solutions' Business Services Division began in Middle Georgia 17 years ago. It started with the acquisition of Acme Business Products in Macon. The home office for its Southern Marketplace is still located in Macon and manages over 15 branch locations in four different states.

IKON has grown from a simple copier company to a worldwide business communications solutions provider. The company's goal is to be able to provide its customers with "total solutions" for the effective communication of their business information. From single copies to complex electronic information exchanges, including network connections and document management, IKON has the expertise to develop the solution that works best!

IKON's products are as diverse as the customers it serves. Major lines offered include Ricoh, Canon, and Oce'. Partnering with its vendors has enabled the company to maintain cost efficiencies that are passed on to customers. Numerous services are offered, and specialized solutions are developed, as customers' needs change.

IKON Business Services provides solutions to customers with a wide range of document processing needs, from the small "start-up" business trying to incorporate digital technology to enable them to grow to the large corporation producing millions of impressions per month. IKON can meet both customers' requirements and all those businesses in between.

IKON's Service Department and Marketing Department are among the most tenured in the industry. They want their employees to enjoy a rewarding work environment—one in which they can learn and grow. Continual training and educational opportunities help build careers and ensure that its people have the expertise to solve problems in this rapidly changing technological age.

IKON encourages its employees to get involved in community activities and participate in charitable organizations. IKON matches, dollar for dollar, eligible monetary contributions made by its employees. It has helped support Little League Teams, local universities such as Mercer and Wesleyan, and has been a major contributor to the American Cancer Society. IKON Business Services is honored to be a part of the Middle Georgia community.

• (top left) IKON's Winning Team, from left: Supply Manager Lisa Dent, Equipment Manager Hunter Squires, Supply Representative Paige Harris, Branch Sales Manager Dylan Veal, Account Representative Kim Bohan, Service Manager Paul Burnam, and Supply Representative Brian Hill.

• (top right) Macon Equipment Sales Team, from left: Dylan Veal, Kim Bohan, and Hunter Squires.

• (right) Macon Supply Sales Team, from left: Paige Harris, Lisa Dent, and Brian Hill.

IOS CAPITAL

IOS Capital (formerly Alco Capital) was established in 1987. Its mission then and today is to provide lease financing for the customers of IKON Office Solutions, one of the world's leading providers of products and services that help businesses communicate.

Since 1987 IOS Capital has grown from $13 million in annual lease funding to over $1.5 billion. Today, the company services a lease portfolio of over 270,000 customers representing $3 billion, positioning the company as one of the largest captive leasing companies in North America.

Located on Bass Road in Macon, IOS Capital's national facility spans nearly 100,000 square feet and now employs over 370 talented individuals from Macon and the surrounding area. It's a far cry from the initial handful of employees and 600 square feet of office space the company started with back in 1987.

The company's original charter was to serve as a back office-processing center. Today it's a full-service leasing company. Functions range from credit, contract review, billing, customer service, collections, and asset recovery, to supporting IKON's national accounts.

According to company President Russ Slack, "Our employees remain IOS Capital's greatest asset as demonstrated by our tremendous growth over the years. Over 600 IKON locations from coast to coast and our immense customer base benefit from our employees' strong work ethic and continuous drive to provide stellar service." In addition to the company's highly spirited employees, IOS Capital remains involved in numerous community programs.

Today, over 70 percent of the products and services sold by IKON are financed through IOS Capital. This high percentage is attributed to the numerous benefits of leasing, which include protection against obsolescence, income tax advantages, affordability, and protection of existing credit lines. Additionally, IOS Capital has a leading-edge IT department and data center offering customers innovative products, which include setting industry standards for customized billing and Copy Management programs. On an annualized basis, IOS Capital generates nearly 3 million invoices and manages 1.6 million telephone calls. The financial contribution the company provides IKON has grown to be very significant.

Despite the growth and success, IOS Capital continues to invest in its infrastructure, including ongoing training for its employees. The types of equipment and services the company has financed over the years may have changed, but the employees of IOS Capital understand that their relationship with customers is as much a reflection of IKON as the sales professionals they support nationwide.

Slack also stated, "Our organization is always in a state of self-improvement to provide a rewarding work environment for our employees as well as to seek enhanced methods to better serve our customers. We are all very proud to be a part of IKON and to call Macon our home." ❋

• (top) IOS Capital's dynamic financing solutions offer customers from coast to coast a seamless method of acquiring IKON's products and services.

• (left) IOS Capital's Leader Team continuously seeks out innovative methods to enhance service levels to IKON's customers.

THE GREATER MACON CHAMBER OF COMMERCE

The Greater Macon Chamber of Commerce, established over 35 years ago, is a voluntary membership organization of the business community. A private, non-profit, tax-paying corporation, the Chamber is dedicated to the advancement of economic, civic, and cultural growth in Middle Georgia. The Chamber's aim is also to promote continuous improvement of the Greater Macon area as a place in which to live and conduct business.

The Greater Macon Chamber of Commerce unites hundreds of businesses and professional firms and has a membership of more than 1,400 member businesses. Hundreds of active volunteers work on numerous committees that assist the Chamber in fulfilling its mission. The Chamber is an organization where people come together to get information, share ideas, and develop solutions to improve the business environment and, ultimately, the quality of life in Middle Georgia.

The Chamber's primary focuses are economic development, government affairs, and education. Through its focus on economic development, the Chamber is dedicated to industry recruitment and support for existing industry, which creates more than 80 percent of all new jobs. The Macon Economic Development Commission (MEDC), which is funded two-thirds by the Chamber, is the marketing arm of the Chamber to business and industrial prospects. A partnership of government and private industry, MEDC is also very active in assisting companies and their employees in making the move and becoming acclimated to Macon and Bibb County. Macon consistently adds more jobs than any other metropolitan area in Georgia with the exception of Atlanta

The Government Affairs committee seeks to ensure that the Chamber is an effective political force in the community and that it represents the Chamber's membership on all appropriate matters to all government agencies—on local, state, and federal levels. The Chamber promotes representation of the business community at public government meetings, communication of government developments to the business community, and support for public referendums that benefit business or help improve infrastructure for economic development.

One of the Government Affairs Committee's biggest efforts is the annual Taste of Macon/Macon Day, which takes place while the Georgia General Assembly is in session. Five teams—representing economic development, education, government, tourism, transportation, and Leadership Macon—meet with various state agencies and visit the House and Senate chambers in Atlanta. Many local restaurants participate in Taste of Macon, which is given by Macon's local delegation in honor of the General Assembly. This event, which

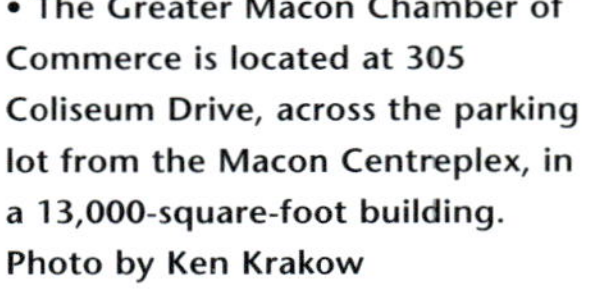

• The Greater Macon Chamber of Commerce is located at 305 Coliseum Drive, across the parking lot from the Macon Centreplex, in a 13,000-square-foot building. Photo by Ken Krakow

continues to grow steadily each year, had an attendance of approximately 1,900 in 2000.

The Chamber challenges member businesses to become more involved directly with the improvement and support of education through partnerships with schools, classes, colleges, and universities. The Education Committee's purpose is to ensure that the Chamber offers the maximum support for education in Macon and Bibb County, in both public and private schools. The education effort supports the mission of the Macon 2000 Partnership, which was established as a focus area of the Chamber to improve education in the Bibb County Public School system.

The Greater Macon Chamber of Commerce offers many other services to its membership, including the basic areas of access, information, representation, and solutions. Business networking is provided through events such as Business After Hours, volunteer committees, and new member breakfasts. The Chamber also hosts monthly professional development seminars and services on subjects such as customer service, legal issues facing businesses, management techniques, and marketing. The Drugs Don't Work Program has been successful in reducing drug abuse in the work place by raising drug awareness with employers, thereby saving them considerably on their workers' compensation expenses. The Chamber's Lead List Program provides useful information for newcomers, and many companies find the Chamber's membership directory useful.

Another focus of the Chamber is paying attention to the concerns of existing industry and the community. The Chamber assists industrial parks in holding regular meetings to encourage neighboring industries to share mutual concerns and provide representation in the areas of policy development and infrastructure improvements. The Chamber also provides a multitude of information resources including demographics information, mailing lists, legislative updates, transportation improvement updates, government meeting reports, surveys, and access to numerous other information and research organizations.

Through the years, the Chamber has been a catalyst for the creation of many organizations that are now large enough to support themselves. Some of these organizations include the Macon/Bibb County Convention & Visitors Bureau, Career Women's Network, the Better Business Bureau, Macon Arts Alliance, Macon 2000 Partnership, Macon Progress, Leadership Macon, the Downtown Council, the Cherry Blossom Festival, and the annual Jubilee Street Parties. The Chamber also provided incubator support for the Georgia Music Hall of Fame and the Georgia Sports Hall of Fame—both of which are located in downtown Macon.

The Greater Macon Chamber of Commerce has been historically involved in many projects for the Macon area, including the establishment of Robins Air Force Base in 1940 and the revitalization of the downtown business area. The Chamber was instrumental in pulling together and getting the funding approved for the new music district, which includes the Georgia Music Hall of Fame and the Georgia Sports Hall of Fame, the Cherry Street Plaza, and the Music Plaza.

Other downtown Macon projects supported by the Chamber include the Christmas Lights Program, which draws visitors from outlying areas, and the Police Bicycle Patrol, a valuable deterrent to crime. A new event, which was first sponsored by the Chamber in 1999 and was attended by over 2,000 people that first year, is Taste of Downtown.

In 1998, the Chamber was able to retire its debt and undergo a refurbishment of its building through a capital campaign. A private organization funded 100 percent by member dues, the Chamber is now able to operate on a break-even budget.

The Greater Macon Chamber of Commerce is located at 305 Coliseum Drive, across the parking lot from the Macon Centreplex, in a 13,000-square-foot building. Providing space and services to four other community organizations, the Chamber acts as a central agency with the purpose of improving business, the business environment, and building a better community to serve the needs of the member businesses. ❋

• The Chamber's boardroom was renovated in 1996. Photo by Ken Krakow

SUNTRUST BANK, MIDDLE GEORGIA

SunTrust heads into the new millennium with over a century of banking service to the people of Macon and Middle Georgia. Promising a firm commitment to financial stability, community involvement, and concern for customers when it opened its doors in downtown Macon those many years ago, SunTrust has continued with its pledge to those same business ideas in the year 2001.

Chartered as Continental Trust Company Bank in December of 1890, the bank merged with Macon National Bank in 1930 to become The First National Bank and Trust Company in Macon. Fifty-one years later, the bank's name changed to Trust Co. Bank. In 1995, the name changed to SunTrust.

As one of the oldest banks in Macon, SunTrust boasts 12 branches in Macon and 5 in nearby Warner Robins. The two in-store branches at Publix on Tom Hill Sr. Boulevard in North Macon and Publix on Russell Parkway in Warner Robins offer extended banking hours for SunTrust customers.

In November 1998, SunTrust merged with Crestar Financial of Richmond, Virginia, creating the ninth largest banking institution in the United States. "Even though we're the ninth largest bank in the country, we deliver service like a hometown bank to the Macon community," said James B. Patton, who became the president and CEO of SunTrust Bank, Middle Georgia, on February 1, 2000.

(top) The Board of Directors of SunTrust Bank, Middle Georgia. Pictured from left: First row: Reginald R. Trice, John D. Nations, Tracy Voyles (acting secretary), James B. Patton, Lil Cross Davis, Dr. Nora Kizer Bell, J. Alan Neal, Albert P. Reichert, Sr. Second row: Edward B. James, Jr., Leland Jackson, Ronald R. Frost, Robert L. Dickey, III, Wallace C. Hogan, Eugene C. Dunwody, Third row: Neil W. Propst, William M. Matthews, Steven L. Kruger, Timothy K. Adams, W. Carter Bates, III, George E. Youmans, Jr., George M. Israel, III. Not pictured: Alvin M. Koplin, Jr., Emmet G. McKenzie, Jr., Elmo A. Richardson, Jr., William L. Tift, MD, Frank W. Walthall, III, Floyd B. Williams.

(right) SunTrust Bank, Middle Georgia, Main Office—606 Cherry Street, Macon, Georgia.

Patton, who has been with SunTrust for almost 20 years, came to Macon in 1992 as executive vice president and senior lending officer. Very active in the community, he represents Ward five on Macon City Council and serves as chairman of United Way of Central Georgia. The new president and CEO of SunTrust attends First Presbyterian Church and is Chairman of the Board of Trustees of First Presbyterian Day School. He is a member of the 2000 Class of Leadership Georgia, serves on the board of Leadership Macon, and is a member of the Rotary Club of Macon.

SunTrust Banks, Inc., is an Atlanta-based super-regional bank holding company with assets of more than $100 billion, and $135 billion in trust assets. The company's 1,100 offices, with 1,800 ATMs, located in six states and the District of Columbia provide a wide range of personal, corporate, and institutional financial services.

SunTrust Bank, Middle Georgia, has $721 million in assets and $1.4 billion in trust assets. A local board of directors assists in business development and general oversight of the bank as well as serves as an important advisor in executing SunTrust's strategy of maintaining local focus in its banking business.

SunTrust is a full service bank offering a variety of products and services in addition to numerous checking, savings, and money market accounts, along with portfolio banking and active investor accounts. A new service to customers is Internet Banking, which provides a banking experience to customers that also includes the ability to pay bills on the Internet. The new PC Banking is designed for both commercial and individual customers.

Mortgage lending serves customers whether they are financing a new home or refinancing an existing home. The mortgage department offers a wide variety of financing options including fixed rate mortgages, adjustable rate mortgages, adjustable home loan programs, and construction loans. SunTrust offers second mortgages and equity lines.

Commercial banking services are available for all commercial customers—large or small—for all their banking needs. To coincide with these commercial banking services, SunTrust's Treasury Management Services offers commercial clients efficient solutions for managing disbursements, collections, information reporting, and investments.

Private Client Services helps clients plan for financial success through all phases of life (education, family, retirement) through the use of various investment options. These options include mutual funds, stocks and bonds, and fixed and variable annuities.

Stability and longevity have been the hallmarks of SunTrust throughout its rich history. Since establishing its presence in Macon in 1890, the bank, whose mission is "to initiate and strengthen client relationships by providing total financial solutions, superior value, and outstanding service quality at a high return to its shareholders," has relied upon its customers for success.

As strong community advocates, SunTrust Bank, Middle Georgia's president, officers, and employees support numerous volunteer efforts within the Middle Georgia area. In addition to monetary support, employees participate and are active leaders in such charity organizations and civic endeavors as Relay for Life, Christmas in April, United Way of Central Georgia, and the Greater Macon Chamber of Commerce.

SunTrust's team-based culture contributes to its reputation as "being the best," according to its many, many customers. This team-based culture leads to innovation and continual improvement in services, products, processes, and people.

With its many years of service and its many longtime employees and customers, SunTrust has shown its commitment to—and success at—offering the finest of all banking services. ❋

(top) James B. Patton, president and CEO, SunTrust Bank, Middle Georgia.

(left) Kathryn H. Dennis, senior vice president and private client services manager, SunTrust Bank, Middle Georgia.

DS*ATLANTIC*/TRIBBLE & RICHARDSON

Tribble & Richardson was founded in 1970 by Elmo A. Richardson Jr. and Hiram L. Tribble Sr. and began operations in a small building on Ingleside Avenue with a staff of six. In 1975, with 25 employees, the company moved to a new, 4,800-square-foot building on Pierce Avenue. In 1986, it moved to its current location, a 41,000-square-foot, breathtaking reflective-glass office building at 4875 Riverside Drive.

In 1997, Tribble & Richardson merged with DS*Atlantic* Corporation, a Raleigh, North Carolina-based company. DS*Atlantic* was established in 1979 and provides full-service engineering, architectural, and land surveying services. Elmo A. Richardson Jr. is chairman of the board and CEO of DS*Atlantic* Corporation and Samuel W. Hayes serves as president and chief operating officer. The merger of these two strong companies resulted in a multidisciplined firm offering the resources of over 380 employees in nine offices located in five states, making DS*Atlantic* one of the largest E/A firms in the Southeast. "Our mission 'to provide excellence in professional services for the built environment, enhance the quality of life, and protect the public welfare' is the core of our success and longevity," says Richardson. "We will continue to maintain careful attention to environmental protection, a person-to-person approach with our customers and employees, and a philosophy of quality and timely service."

DS*Atlantic*/Tribble & Richardson has a long and distinguished history of providing professional consulting services in the areas of architectural design; environmental and solid waste management; sanitary, transportation, and general civil engineering; and surveying. "We work primarily for local, state, and federal governments, as well as corporations, industries, educational institutions, developers, and the financial community," said Richardson, "with most of our work being centered around city, county, and state governments. Infrastructure planning is vitally important to these clients to maintain an adequate supply of potable water and wastewater treatment capacity to satisfy the ever-expanding demands of their communities. We provide consulting and design services for water systems, water treatment facilities, water resources, and wastewater treatment and sewerage systems." DS*Atlantic*/Tribble & Richardson's engineers use state-of-the-art technology and computer modeling to project future demands in order to adequately design water distribution and sewage collection systems to meet the needs of municipal clients.

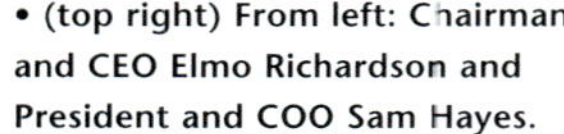

• (top right) From left: Chairman and CEO Elmo Richardson and President and COO Sam Hayes.

• (below) Raw Water Pumping Station for Macon Water Authority's Town Creek Water Treatment Plant.

"We've been involved in the design and construction of major infrastructure improvements in the Macon and Bibb County area," said Richardson. In 1994, the company completed the planning, design, and construction of the Town Creek Reservoir—a 640-acre water supply project—for the Macon Water Authority. In 1999, the firm received the Consulting Engineers Council of Georgia's Engineering Excellence Award for the Town Creek Wetland Mitigation Project, which successfully replaced the wetlands that were impacted by the construction of the new reservoir. Future plans for the mitigation site are to incorporate it into the Ocmulgee Heritage Greenway.

Also, construction is nearing completion on the Raw Water Pumping Station located at the Macon Water Authority's new Water Treatment Plant. DS*Atlantic*/Tribble & Richardson designed this 90-million gallon-per-day pumping facility that is adjacent to the reservoir and wetland mitigation sites.

DS*Atlantic*/Tribble & Richardson's expertise also extends into the area of transportation engineering. Projects include transportation planning, environmental impact statements, field surveys, utility relocation, roadway and bridge design, and intersection improvements. "We're involved in a number of major road projects for local governments as well as for various departments of transportation in several states," Richardson said.

The firm's Architectural Services Department has just completed the design of the new Georgia National Fairgrounds and Agricenter Multipurpose and Exhibit Building. The 70,000-square-foot facility is a signature structure for the fair complex. Construction began in April 2000.

A good example of the firm's full-service capabilities is a project currently underway with Ronald McDonald House Charities of Central Georgia, Inc. DS*Atlantic*/Tribble & Richardson is responsible for the design, site planning, and surveying for the Ronald McDonald House. This "house" will provide a refuge for families from outside the Middle Georgia Area that need a comfortable and conveniently located place to stay while their seriously ill children receive medical care at the Medical Center of Central Georgia.

Richardson's firm and its staff are actively involved in various civic and community activities. "We encourage participation in our professional and community activities," Richardson said. "The community has given a lot to us, and we're trying to return this the best we can. We've been very active not only in local organizations, but also in state and national organizations."

Elmo A. Richardson Jr. has served as chairman of the board of the Greater Macon Chamber of Commerce. He has also served as president of the Consulting Engineers Council of Georgia and as president of the Museum of Arts & Sciences. A graduate of the Georgia Institute of Technology, he is a registered Civil Engineer and Land Surveyor and is a technical advisor to the Georgia Regional Transportation Authority. With over 40 years of experience in all phases of civil, environmental, and sanitary engineering, Richardson has been involved with the planning and design of water resource projects throughout the Southeast.

DS*Atlantic*/Tribble & Richardson has a history that demonstrates its commitment to and accountability for the long-term success of projects. The firm relies heavily on repeat business from satisfied customers. "Hiram Tribble and I also felt that our staff should be number one and should always be treated fairly. Our firm has retained these basic philosophies through the years," Richardson said.

"We feel very fortunate to have been a part of many major developments in this area over the past 30 years," said Richardson. "I'm very excited about the future, and I have great expectations for the next 30 years. Changes in our profession are visible, but our history attests that the need for quality and timely service for our clients endures." ❋

• (top) Water Treatment Plant for Henry County Water and Sewerage Authority.

• (left) Georgia National Fairgrounds Multipurpose and Exhibit Building.

FIRST DATA CORPORATION

MOVING THE WORLD'S MONEY

For decades, First Data Corporation has helped shape the financial services and payments industries. Today, First Data helps move the world's money. Every time someone pays for something by credit or debit card, over the Internet, by check, or by wire transfer—First Data is there. As the leader in electronic commerce and payment services, Atlanta-based First Data Corporation (NYSE:FDC) serves more than two million merchant locations, 1,400 card issuers, and millions of consumers—making it easier, faster, and more secure for people and businesses to buy goods and services.

First Data subsidiaries include Western Union and TeleCheck. Western Union enables consumers and businesses to securely transfer money or make payments using money orders and other electronic systems. Western Union is credited with introducing the age of electronic commerce by launching the first electronic money transfer service in 1871. Today, the company is an industry leader, moving funds in minutes through approximately 94,000 agent locations in 185 countries and territories. Western Union also markets more than a quarter billion money orders every year.

TeleCheck Services Inc. is the world's largest check acceptance company. It provides a broad range of check guarantee, check verification, and collection services to merchants and financial institutions. With the most sophisticated system in the industry, TeleCheck continues to make checks easier and safer for merchants to accept and for consumers to use. Over the past three decades, TeleCheck has expanded to nearly $155 billion in annual check volume representing more than 3.1 billion transactions, serving more than 228,000 customers worldwide.

First Data's roots can be traced back to Omaha, Nebraska, in 1971 when a small company was created to process credit cards for an association of seven Midwest banks. First Data Resources, as the startup company was called, led to the creation of payment services leader First Data Corporation and made a name for itself as the world's largest transaction processor.

Today, First Data Resources is the credit and debit card processing division of First Data Corporation and works with more than 1,400 clients who issue credit, debit, retail, commercial, and oil card products. As the industry leader, First Data's card issuing business:

- manages 260 million accounts around the world.
- handles credit and debit card transactions for millions of consumers 24 hours-a-day, 7 days-a-week, 365 days a year.
- performs off-line debit card processing for more than 56 million debit cards issued by over 500 financial institutions.
- processes approximately 7 billion transactions worldwide every year.

Internationally, First Data has established a presence in major markets. FDR Limited (FDRL), based in the United Kingdom, is a leading credit and debit card transaction processor in Europe, serving the needs of over 50 financial institutions and 450,000 merchant locations in the U.K., Germany, and Spain. In Australia, First Data is the largest independent electronic funds transfer network, providing EFT and card processing services for more than 350 clients. Through its Latin American division, First Data provides transaction-processing services to financial institutions within Mexico and Latin America. In 2000, First Data entered the Canadian and Japanese markets and continues to seek opportunities to expand into other markets internationally.

First Data Resources' Delivery Operations handles all printing, inserting, and mailing of credit card statements, letters, and reports for card issuing financial and retail institution clients. The operations are open 24-hours-a-day, 7-days-a-week. The facilities produce printed material on behalf of card issuers, including: bankcard and merchant statements, letters to cardholders, first activity and past due notices to cardholders, and various other reports.

Using a variety of high-speed laser printers, millions of credit card statements are printed each day. These statements are folded and inserted into envelopes along with any required inserts, utilizing over 200 inserting machines. The in-house Zip (Code) Sorting facility receives and sorts letters, statements, and other credit card products that are forwarded to the U.S. Postal Service for distribution.

INTERESTING FACTS

- Together, Omaha and Macon Delivery Operations facilities mail over five million pieces of mail on an average workday.
- First Data's Omaha and Macon operations combined produce and mail 100 million statements each month, making First Data one of the largest Zip (Code) Sorting facilities in the United States.
- First Data has one of the largest laser printing operations in the United States. Its Omaha and Macon operations together use a total of 63 high-speed continuous-form simplex and duplex printers and 9 cut sheet printers.
- First Data produces a total of 178 million feet of printed material a month from its Omaha and Macon facilities, including bankcard and merchant statements, and financial institution reports.

IN MACON

Through an acquisition, First Data came to the Macon community in November 1999. The facility, located in Northwest Macon, became part of First Data Resources Delivery Operations organization, which includes other print, mail, and plastics embossing facilities in Omaha, Nebraska, and Chesapeake, Virginia. About 225 employees in Macon joined First Data's 29,000 employees around the world.

First Data is an active member of The Greater Macon Chamber of Commerce and is a corporate partner in the Macon community and surrounding area. ❋

WACHOVIA CORPORATION

• Main office at 484 Mulberry Street.

Wachovia Corporation, an interstate financial holding company with dual headquarters in Atlanta, Georgia, and Winston-Salem, North Carolina, serves regional, national, and international markets. Its member companies offer personal, corporate, trust, and institutional financial services.

The principal banking subsidiary, Wachovia Bank, N.A., provides a wide range of services to consumers and small businesses through nearly 700 offices and 1,400 ATMs in five states: Florida, Georgia, North Carolina, South Carolina, and Virginia.

Wachovia serves corporate customers through its locations in the Southeast, Chicago, New York City, London, and Sao Paulo, and through its representatives in Hong Kong, Tokyo, New York City, and Grand Cayman. Its operations centers are located in Atlanta, Georgia; Charlotte, Raleigh, and Winston-Salem, North Carolina; Columbia, South Carolina; and Charlottesville, Virginia.

Wachovia has lockbox remittance processing centers, a major credit card operation, credit life and general insurance companies, and residential mortgage loan services in several states.

As of June 30, 2000, Wachovia had total assets of $70.8 billion, deposits of $42.6 billion, and a market capitalization of $13.7 billion. As of December 31, 1999, Wachovia had total trust assets of approximately $132.7 billion under administration.

Wachovia Capital Markets, a division of Wachovia Securities Inc., provides a wide range of services to commercial customers. These services include investment banking, merchant banking, structured finance, institutional sales and training, debt capital markets, and risk management. Wachovia's Treasury Services division provides a wide range of cash management services and is consistently ranked as a leading, high-quality provider.

The nation's 12th largest credit card issuer, Wachovia Bank Card Services operates and manages 6.7 million credit card accounts with outstandings averaging $8.4 billion. It is nationally recognized for its low-rate card offerings. Wachovia Merchant Services, providing business customers with bank card processing services for every major credit or debit card, offers a full complement of related and supporting services. Wachovia Merchant Services serviced more than 30,000 customer locations and processed $6.5 billion in transaction volume in 1999.

Wachovia provides full-service brokerage services and private banking/trust services. Financial and investment counselors are located in offices in several states. Wachovia provides discount brokerage services through Wachovia Investments Direct and also offers the Wachovia Funds, a family of proprietary mutual funds. Private Financial Advisor and Wachovia subsidiary companies serve clients with more extensive wealth management needs.

The first major bank to offer simple interest consumer loans, Wachovia also was a pioneer of variable-rate credit cards and the adjustable-rate mortgage, which became an industry model. It is consistently ranked among the world's safest banks and is noted for the high quality of its treasury services. According to a recent national poll by PSI Global, Wachovia was the only commercial banking company ranked by millionaires among the top 10 wealth management institutions.

In 1985, First Atlanta Corporation and The Wachovia Corporation merged to form First Wachovia Corporation. The combined company was renamed Wachovia Corporation in 1991. First Atlanta was renamed Wachovia Bank of Georgia, N.A., in 1991, and Wachovia Bank, N.A., in 1997. Wachovia completed a number of other mergers in the last decade of the last century and the organization now has more than 21,300 employees.

As a corporate citizen, Wachovia commits funding and other resources to improve opportunity and quality of life in such areas as economy, development, education, health care, and the arts. Wachovia is looking forward to continuing its proud legacy of excellence in banking services and community outreach in the new millennium. ❋

IJL WACHOVIA

One of the nation's largest regional full-service brokerage firms, IJL Wachovia has over 450 financial consultants serving more than 65 communities in North Carolina, South Carolina, Virginia, Georgia, and Tennessee. Locally, the Macon and Warner Robins offices are staffed with a total of 14 financial consultants and 8 support personnel.

A full-service brokerage firm, IJL Wachovia is made up of a dedicated team of investment support professionals who specialize in a full range of investment services. As a division of Wachovia Securities, Inc., the firm draws on the vast resources of Wachovia Corporation, one of the nation's largest banking companies, which operates more than 750 offices and has $64 billion in assets and $41 billion in deposits.

Wachovia Securities, Inc. offers a full range of financial brokerage and investment banking services. With its in-depth knowledge of the fast-growing and dynamic Southeast, IJL Wachovia provides its clients with a window to its hometown region. IJL Wachovia's expertise also encompasses the broader national financial scenes, helping provide clients with a comprehensive investment vision.

IJL Wachovia knows the difficulty investors have sorting through the tens of thousands of investment alternatives—stocks, bonds, mutual funds, and nontraditional investment offerings. These options are made even more difficult by changing tax laws, market volatility, interest rate fluctuations, and the impact of complex international influences. IJL Wachovia helps investors make sense of their choices. It carefully assesses a client's personal circumstances, financial situation, investment timeline, and tolerance for risk. Then, it helps investors design a cohesive investment program that is personally tailored.

In order to do this, IJL Wachovia examines the realm of investment products and services, searching for effective ways to help meet each investor's particular needs. At the same time, the company draws upon its significant resources, ranging from timely research data to proven investment strategies.

At IJL Wachovia, investors are analyzed objectively, focusing sharply on their best interests. Recommendations are then based on the investment's intrinsic merit—not on a predetermined agenda. Throughout all this, the professionals at IJL Wachovia remain committed to one principal objective: helping their investors achieve their financial goals.

IJL Wachovia offers more than just objective advice on traditional investments. It also provides comprehensive financial and estate planning, professional investment management consulting services, premium cash management services, portfolio evaluation programs, and personal and corporate trusts. Other services provided include sophisticated risk management strategies, retirement plan design and support, and special programs geared toward the needs of small- to middle-market companies.

IJL Wachovia is known for its commitment to its clients. That is why the company works so hard to build a lasting bond with its investors—a meaningful relationship based upon mutual trust. ❋

CORE MANAGEMENT RESOURCES GROUP

Core Management Resources Group, Inc., (CMRG) is a customer-driven, service organization providing a full range of employee benefit consulting, administration, and technology solutions for employers and other entities. The Core group of companies is positioned to provide leading-edge technology and services that will compete with any of the larger specialized companies in the nation. The people of Core believe that the unique needs of each customer should define the relationship between Core and its clients. The guiding principle of the company is that service, and maintaining up-to-date technology, should never be sacrificed for growth alone.

Under the direct leadership of Tom O. Wagoner, president and CEO, Core Management Resources Group, Inc., serves as a holding company for five other Core companies. Founded in 1979, Core Management Resources, Inc., is the original Core company; Core Administrative Services, Inc., serves as a third-party administrator for self-funded health, dental, vision, disability, and pension plans; Core Health Services, Inc., is the pre-certification, utilization review, and large-case management arm of Core; Core Risk Management Services, Inc., adds property and casualty consulting to its array of services; and Core Advanced Technology, Inc., has written and maintains its own proprietary software for electronically transferring medical claims from the provider to the payer.

During 1999, Core Management Resources Group, Inc., embarked upon a major project to develop a new software system that would help move the company into the 21st century. In doing so, the company brought together a cadre of bright, energetic, and creative people, and together they embraced the philosophy of providing outstanding service in an environment marked by both "high-tech" and "high touch." This group has worked to achieve the highest standards of performance and integrity, reflecting Core's commitment to being the best business solution for helping clients enhance their operations and expand their profits.

CMRG's new revolutionary health management benefits administration system, CoreLink, is a fully integrated, Web-based benefit and human resource administration package for managing benefits' eligibility, enrollment, utilization, billing, reporting, and employee communications. With direct electronic access by CoreLink, Core provides a full range of benefit functions, including real-time eligibility, on-line enrollments, account maintenance, electronic billing, and electronic funds transfer payment options. CMRG's vision of the future includes an information system that will link employees, employers, doctors, hospitals, and pharmacists together with the click of a mouse. Core's integrated approach also provides accessibility to on-site nurses and case managers to answer the most basic health-care questions or to assess in managing catastrophic disease care.

Emerging technologies will transform not only the delivery, but also the quality, of health care and health-care infrastructures as recognized today. Technology will help to address the issues of privacy standards, eligibility, portability, coordination of benefit issues, and the uninsured. The Core Management Resources Group expects to be a significant partner with employers, governments, payers, and groups of providers in addressing the technology and the programs needed to undergird an effective health-care system.

For more information visit Core Management Resources Group's Web site at www.coremrg.com. ❋

• Under the direct leadership of Tom O. Wagoner, president and CEO, Core Management Resources Group, Inc., serves as a holding company for five other Core companies.

GEOTECHNICAL & ENVIRONMENTAL CONSULTANTS, INC.

Geotechnical & Environmental Consultants, Inc. (GEC), formerly Geosciences, Inc., is an engineering consulting firm, which was founded in 1991 in Macon. It currently has offices in both Macon and Columbus, Georgia. While the initial focus of GEC was in the performance of geotechnical engineering and construction quality control testing services, the variety of services has evolved into a full range of property environmental services. Headed by President and Senior Engineer Thomas E. Driver, P.E., the GEC staff, which now includes 38 engineers, geologists, biologists, environmental specialists, engineering technicians, and secretarial staff members, is dedicated to providing its clientele with high-quality, cost-effective, timely professional services, offering practical solutions to engineering problems.

Geotechnical engineering services form the roots of GEC. The firm works to determine and provide recommendations for the geotechnical aspects of a proposed development or to help determine the causes of a problem or failure in a building or pavement system. Geotechnical studies typically address such issues as site preparation techniques; foundation, wall, and pavement system design; anticipated building settlement; and slope stability, as well as dam design, design of Construction Monitoring Plans for stormwater control, and the assesment of sites for on-site waste disposal systems.

GEC strongly believes that the use of a third party consultant to provide construction quality control (QC) services is essential to the overall quality of a project. GEC has a talented staff of engineering technicians and field engineers trained in the performance of these services. Typical services include soil density, asphalt, and concrete, mortar, and grout testing; and foundation, masonry, roofing,

structural-steel, and fire-proofing inspection among others. Additional non-traditional services include floor flatness profiling, NPDES storm water sampling, and inspection of erosion control devices. All of GEC's technicians are required to be American Concrete Institute (ACI) certified. The geotechnical and construction quality control services are supported by GEC's in-house soil, asphalt, and concrete laboratories.

GEC provides a wide variety of environmental services, ranging from the assessment of properties prior to site acquisition and underground storage tank consultation services to the design of groundwater remediation systems and other services related to the design, operation, and monitoring of solid waste facilities. Property-related environmental services include determining whether or not there have been activities on or adjacent to a property that would create a cause for environmental concern through the performance of Phase I and II Environmental Site Assessments, asbestos and lead based paint inspection, and radon testing. For solid waste facilities, GEC provides services that assist clients from the site characterization, design, and permitting stages through closure and post closure monitoring. These services range from pre-permitting geotechnical studies to the performance of construction quality control testing during construction and sampling, testing, and reports of groundwater required during operation. Industrial environmental services include the design of Stormwater (SWPPP) and Spill (SPCC) plans as well as occupational safety consultation.

Some of the major projects that GEC has worked on include the Macon Water Authority's Town Creek Plant, Georgia Sports Hall of Fame, Tubman African American Museum, Bibb County Public School Projects, the B-1 Bomber Beddown, Best Buy Distribution Center, Macon Mall expansion, Quad Graphics Printing facility, Port Columbus Civil War Naval Museum, Columbus River Walk, Swift Textiles Mill, South Commons Softball Complex, and Florida Rock Quarry.

GEC provides a wide variety of services, and its staff believes in the principal of providing quality, timely, and professional products to its clientele. This has been the strongest factor in its growth. GEC is proud to be a part of the growth and excitement of the Middle Georgia community. ❋

• (top) Thomas E. Driver, P.E., President of GEC.

• (left) Subsurface evaluation being performed for the future Tubman African American Museum.
Photos by Ken Krakow

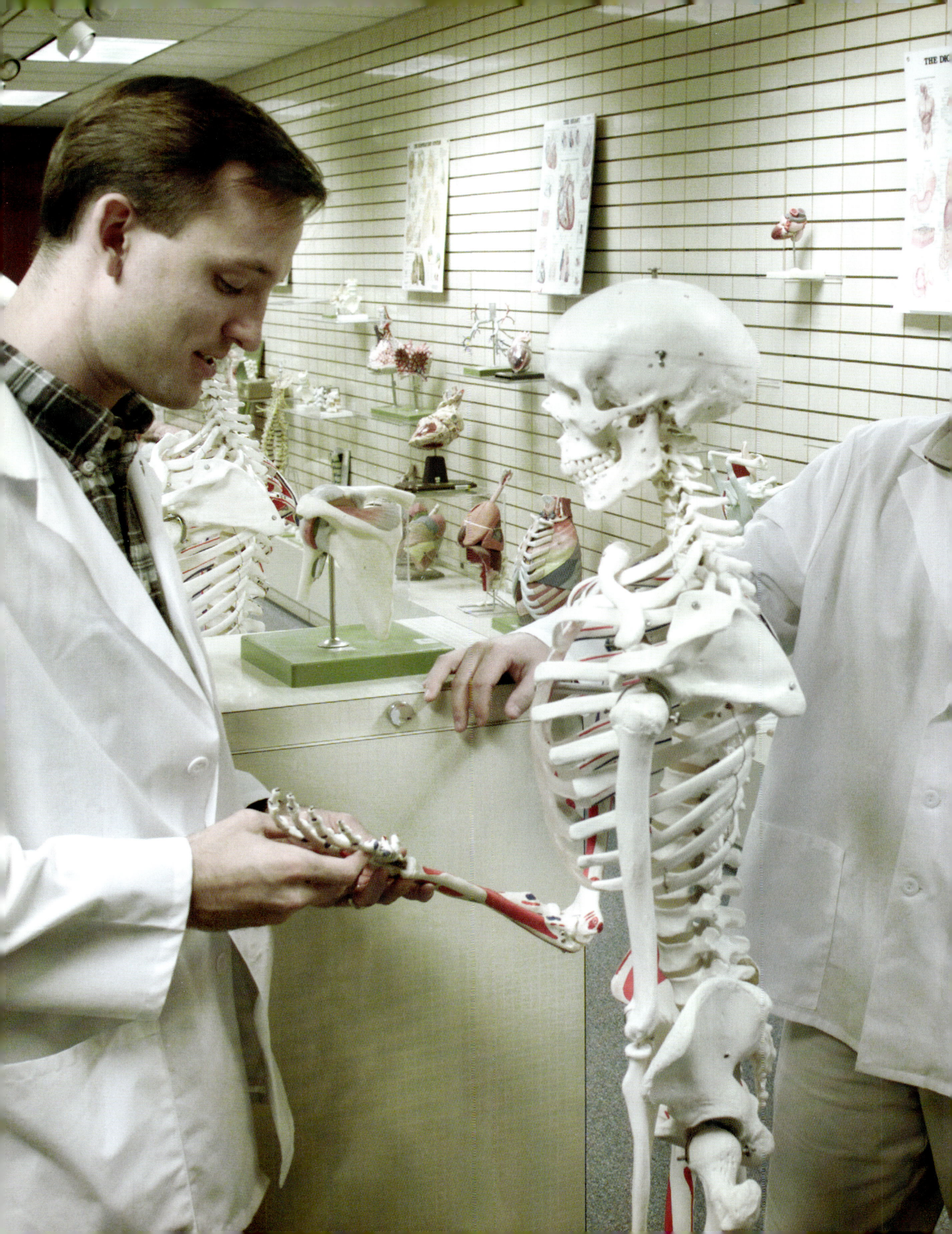

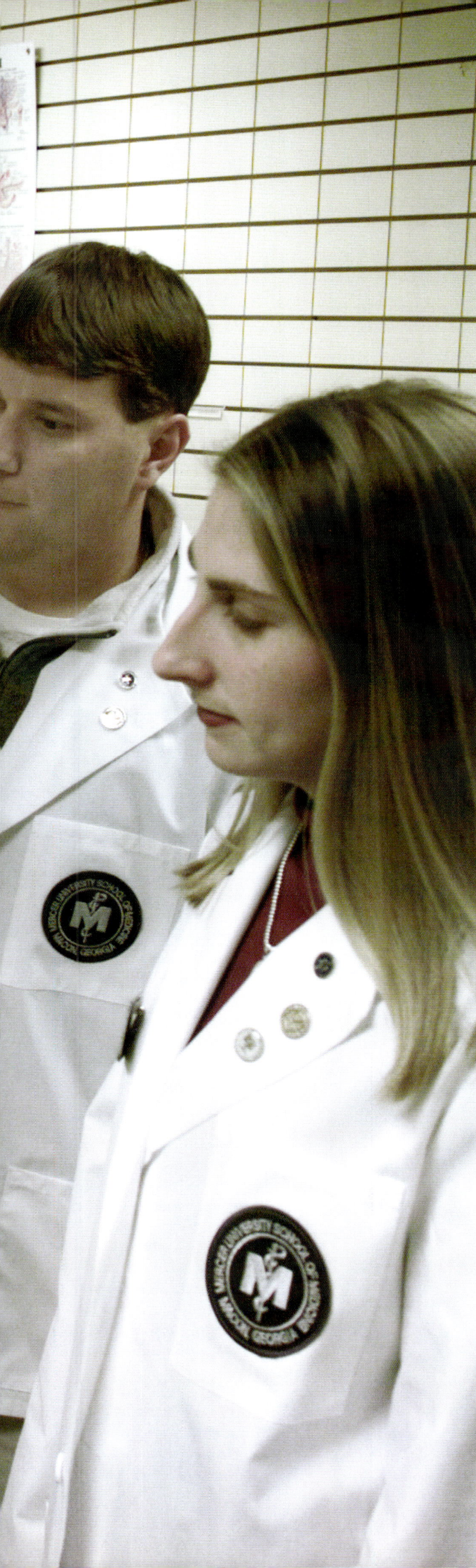

CHAPTER ELEVEN

11

Education

Photo by Ken Krakow

MERCER UNIVERSITY

Dating back to 1871 when Macon's civic leaders recruited Mercer University to move from the tiny hamlet of Penfield, Georgia, to their bustling city on the Ocmulgee River, Mercer has answered the call.

As industry and commerce increased and Macon grew, Mercer expanded to meet the higher education needs of the city, state, region, and nation. Over the years, Mercer has supplied Macon and Middle Georgia with ministers, lawyers and judges, educators, business leaders, engineers, and physicians. Mercer's growth has matched Macon's expansion, never failing to keep pace with the demand.

This symbiotic relationship has never been more evident than today, as the calendar indicates the start of a new millennium and the evolving local culture demands new skills and innovation.

"Throughout its history, Mercer has exemplified the strong connection between serving the community and learning," said Dr. R. Kirby Godsey, Mercer University President. "It's not just a concept Mercer teaches its students. It's a guiding principle that has been a part of this University since the life of Jesse Mercer. We believe it is important for Mercer to serve Macon and Middle Georgia, and our history bears that out."

• (top) Founded in 1833 in Penfield, Georgia, Mercer University moved to Macon in 1871, at first occupying only the Administration Building, shown here.

• (right) Mercer University enrolls more than 7,400 students and is the only independent university its size in the nation to offer programs in liberal arts, business and economics, education, engineering, law, pharmacy, medicine, nursing, and theology.

When Jesse Mercer founded the University in 1833, it was primarily a liberal arts college. That mission continued when the school moved to Macon. Mercer provided a well-rounded education that allowed Macon and Middle Georgia students to pursue the career of their choice.

It did not take long for Mercer's impact to extend beyond undergraduate education. In 1873, two years after the relocation to Macon, the Walter F. George School of Law was founded and began equipping students to excel in the growing legal community in Middle Georgia.

Because of Macon's central location, state, district, and federal courts were headquartered there, requiring the best young legal minds. Mercer met that need. One of the oldest law schools in the country, the Walter F. George School of Law has performed its mission well, repeatedly earning the Gambrelli Professionalism Award for "depth and excellence" from the American Bar Association.

"The Law School has made a tremendous impact on this community and the state," Dr. Godsey said. "Almost every Georgia community and major firm in Macon or Atlanta has a Mercer law graduate."

For more than 100 years Mercer continued to educate the sons and daughters of Georgia in the liberal arts tradition and through the law school. In 1982, Mercer again answered the call, this time from city and state leaders.

In the 1970s, many Georgia communities were without adequate medical care. Leaders turned to Mercer for the answer. Because Mercer's commitment to medical education was already evident through the merger of the Southern School of Pharmacy in Atlanta with the University in 1959, Mercer was the ideal institution to meet the state's health care need.

"Georgia had many medically underserved communities," Dr. Godsey said. "Hundreds of small towns did not have a physician, forcing people to drive to the metropolitan centers such as Macon, Augusta, or Atlanta for medical care. Recognizing the tremendous need for doctors in those areas, the state legislature provided funding for a mission-specific medical school at Mercer. Now we are one of the nation's foremost medical schools for producing primary care physicians."

Mercer's success in fulfilling its mission is well documented. In 2000, the Medical School received its ninth consecutive award from the American Academy of Family Physicians for making family practice a leading career choice for graduating medical students. Mercer's commitment to its mission is also evident in the fact that 54 percent of Mercer graduates practice medicine in federally designated Health Professional Shortage Areas in Georgia.

In the 1970s and 1980s, Macon experienced increased industry and business growth. Recognizing a need for management training, Mercer in 1984 separated its business and economics department within the College of Liberal Arts and created a business school. The Eugene W. Stetson School of Business and Economics, named for the Mercer alumnus who played key roles in The Coca-Cola Company and Illinois Central Railroad, built its curriculum to include majors in the areas of accounting, computer information systems, economics, finance, and management.

The Business School also introduced a Master of Business Administration degree, filling a much-needed gap in the area of advanced business education in Macon and Middle Georgia. Today, the Stetson School of Business and Economics is one of the largest components of the University, enrolling more than 1,500 students and offering courses in Macon, Atlanta, and Douglas County.

One of Mercer's major business-enrichment programs is the Executive Forum. Established in 1979, the Executive Forum brings the country's most sought-after speakers to Macon and Atlanta to share ideas with local business leaders. The impressive lineup of speakers has included publisher Steve Forbes, Wall Street strategist Louis Rukeyser, news anchor Cokie Roberts, football coach Lou Holtz, political commentator Tim Russert, the Reverend Jesse Jackson, and U.S. Senator Sam Nunn.

"The Executive Forum allows us to touch so many people in the community by exposing them to new ideas and the latest, cutting-edge trends in business and industry," Dr. Godsey said. "It has become Georgia's premier business enrichment program and is the longest continuous program of its kind in the state."

The next chapter of Mercer's call to serve centered on the need for technical and technological expertise in Middle Georgia. In 1985, the commander at Robins Air Force Base, located 15 miles south of Macon, contacted Mercer and expressed a need for qualified engineers to fulfill the base's mission. The local labor pool could not keep pace with the demand for engineers, and a solid, well-rounded engineering program was needed to keep Robins viable.

Mercer responded. The School of Engineering was founded, offering a general engineering bachelor's degree; master's degrees with a variety of specializations including biomedical, computer, environmental, industrial, and mechanical engineering; and a bachelor's degree in environmental systems, industrial management, and technical communication.

The School of Engineering led to the creation of the Mercer Engineering Research Center in Warner Robins in 1987. The Center became the University's formal engineering consulting arm, working with both government and commercial clients.

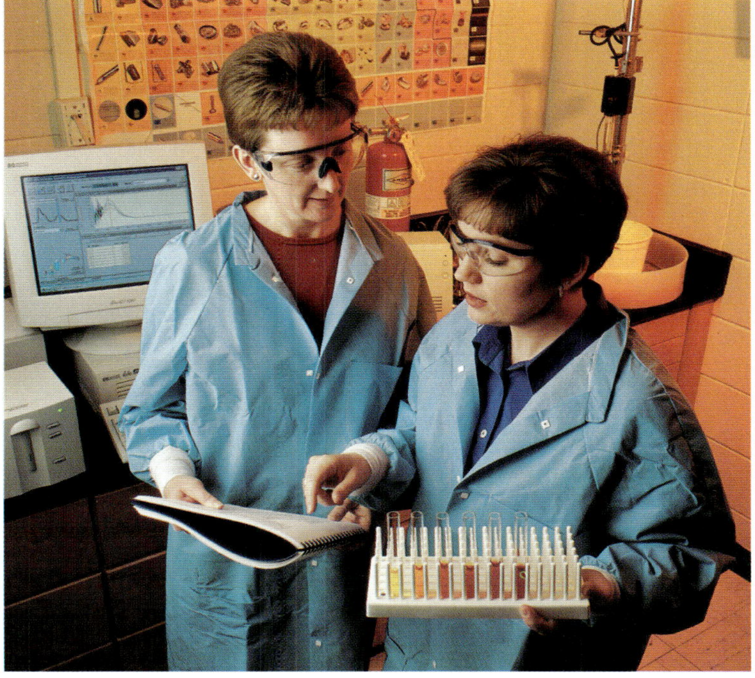

• (top) Mercer's beautiful and historic campus enters the new millennium in the midst of a significant upgrade. The $100 million Campus Improvement Program included an exterior renovation of the Administration Building, shown here, as well as the addition of a University Center, Music Building, on-campus apartments, and a Greek Village, made up of 18 fraternity and sorority houses.

• (left) Chemistry student Karen Sinclair and Dr. Elaine Butler take advantage of Mercer's outstanding laboratory facilities in conducting undergraduate research. Mercer is unique in the number of research opportunities afforded students through the Undergraduate Research Initiative, which was established in 1998.

In the mid-1980s, Tift College, a small, Baptist women's college in Forsyth, Georgia, merged with Mercer, desiring to continue its commitment to educating women. In 1990, the University established the Tift College Scholars Program, one of the University's most distinguished scholastic organizations. Each year, the program awards scholarships to select young women attending Mercer, preserving Tift's heritage, identity, and ideals.

In the 1990s, Mercer turned its attention to helping provide Georgia's young people with a quality education. The shortage of qualified teachers was a major statewide issue. Mercer responded by creating a School of Education in 1995 from its teacher education programs within the University. The largest school at Mercer, the School of Education fills the state's need for highly qualified teachers for kindergarten to high school.

"Educators are one of the greatest resources and greatest needs in Georgia," Dr. Godsey said. "Through the School of Education, Mercer is able to continue the tradition established in the early days of this institution by providing well-trained and well-rounded classroom teachers. This School directly influences the quality of life in Macon and across the state."

Outside the realm of academia, Mercer has contributed a number of arts initiatives benefiting Macon and Middle Georgia. One of only two academic presses in Georgia, Mercer University Press has produced an average of 40 titles a year since 1979. Books range from Southern and religious themes to biographies and memoirs of some of Georgia's most influential leaders.

The University also manages Bibb County's historic Grand Opera House. Because of the University's arts expertise, Mercer stepped forward and put together an attractive and sustainable program for The Grand that includes Broadway shows and musical events.

• (top) Founded in 1873, the Walter F. George School of Law at Mercer is one of the nation's oldest and most respected law schools. It is located on scenic Coleman Hill, overlooking downtown Macon.

• (right) Mercer University fields 14 intercollegiate teams in Division I of the National Collegiate Athletic Association and is a founding member of the Trans America Athletic Conference. Mercer has claimed nine team conference championships and two individual sport conference championships. Mercer has twice won the conference's All-Academic Trophy for having the most student athletes earning a 3.0 grade point average or better.

In 2000, it became the home of the Macon Symphony Orchestra.

The emphasis Mercer has put on the arts in Macon is matched in intensity by the University's efforts at community redevelopment. Mercer has been an active partner in the revitalization of Macon's Huguenin Heights and Central South neighborhoods as well as the downtown business district. As the new millennium begins, Dr. Godsey serves as board president for NewTown Macon, a private organization chartered to attract new development downtown.

Mercer is helping rejuvenate the city by enhancing its campus appearance. The University is progressing on $100 million in construction that includes a Greek Village for fraternities and sororities, on-campus apartments, the University Center for athletic and cultural events, a music building with a state-of-the-art performance auditorium, a Baptist Student Union building, renovations of historic campus buildings, and other landscaping and grounds improvements.

With thriving campuses in Macon and Atlanta, Mercer repeatedly has been ranked among the top colleges and universities in the South. Today, Mercer is the only independent university of its size in the country that combines programs in liberal arts, business, education, engineering, law, medicine, nursing, pharmacy, and theology.

Whether it's an academic program, a qualified work force, an expert or leader, an artistic performance, or a physical presence, Mercer University continues to fulfill the promise of being a committed partner in the growth and future of Macon and Middle Georgia. The new millennium represents a new beginning for the city and the University and a continuation of more than a century of cooperation.

"What's good for Macon is good for Mercer," Dr. Godsey said. "And we believe it's also true that what's good for Mercer is good for Macon. That's why we look to continue our strong ties to Macon and Middle Georgia as we pursue higher levels of achievement and prosperity in the years to come." ❋

• (top) Dr. Stanley Roberts conducts the Mercer Singers in Newton Chapel. In 2001, Mercer's Music Department will move into a state-of-the-art music building that features music technology laboratories and an elegant and acoustically engineered recital hall with a seating capacity of about 200.

• (left) Mercer rededicated and renamed the main library in April 2000 for alumnus and former *Atlanta Journal-Constitution* publisher and Associated Press chairman Jack Tarver. Other notable Mercer alumni are Judge Griffin B. Bell, 72nd Attorney General of the United States; Judge William Augustus Bootle, who ordered the integration of the University of Georgia in 1961; Georgia Secretary of State Cathy Cox; and former newspaper editor and publisher and former president of the National Geographic Society Reg Murphy.

CENTRAL GEORGIA TECHNICAL COLLEGE (CGTC)

For more than three decades, Central Georgia Technical College (CGTC) has been committed to delivering quality, affordable instructional programs that serve the best interests of its students and respond to the area's economic and educational challenges.

CGTC began its partnership with Middle Georgia citizens, businesses, and industry when it was officially established in 1962 as the Macon Area Vocational-Technical School under the direction of the Bibb County Board of Education and Orphanage. Initial construction of the school was completed in 1966 with the first class graduating in August of 1967.

Student enrollment in those early years averaged 200 students per quarter, and students attended one of three locations in Macon. With a name change to Macon Technical Institute in 1987 and a shift to state governance under the Department of Technical and Adult Education in 1989, CGTC now has a burgeoning student population that averages 3,500 credit-hour students per quarter. At the current rate of growth, the college's student population will surpass 5,000 by 2005.

A local Board of Directors was established in 1989 after the transfer to state governance. The 12-member board is representative of the College's service-delivery area, with members from Baldwin, Bibb, Jones, Monroe, Putnam, and Twiggs counties. The State Board of Technical and Adult Education appoints members to the College's Board of Directors. A private foundation was established in 1993 and membership on the Board of Trustees is comprised of community leaders. The Central Georgia Technical College Foundation coordinates the solicitation of funds, grants, and properties from individuals, corporations, government agencies and private sources. The Foundation also provides private funding for capital expansion and improvement, equipment, staff and faculty development, scholarships and endowments.

The growth of Middle Georgia in the decade following the college's inception resulted in an increased demand for the quality educational services that CGTC provides. This required a larger campus to accommodate additional instructional programs, expanding technology, and an influx of students. The current Macon location off Eisenhower Parkway across from Colonial Mall Macon, was completed in 1978; this location offered a consolidated, centrally located Macon campus, expanded instructional capabilities, and potential for growth.

The addition of an Allied Health/Economic Development building, the expansion of laboratories in two buildings, and the purchase of acreage in 1996 by the CGTC Foundation, has given the College a potential campus size of over 100 acres. The pledge to meet the needs of students and the community has been proven in the institute's commitment to expand. A new facility that will include a student center and additional classrooms is also planned for this campus with a projected completion date of July 2002.

Expansions are not limited to the Macon campus. In 1997, CGTC added a 60,000-square-foot Milledgeville facility, which serves as a satellite campus and is designed to meet the needs of students in the Baldwin county service area. Plans are already in place for a major expansion at this location in the next three to five years. A third campus, a 10,000-square-foot training center in Eatonton, is scheduled for completion in 2001. The advanced facilities and the 93 percent job placement rate at CGTC continue to attract students from 35 counties seeking technical certificates, diplomas, associate degrees, and continuing education classes.

Central Georgia Technical College has been a long-time member of the Commission on Occupational Education (COE), a nationally recognized accrediting organization. In 1999, the school was awarded full membership to the Southern Association of Colleges and Schools, Commission on Colleges (SACS/COC). Both accreditations help to support the College's vision of a seamless educational process that allows students to progress from high school to post-secondary training and on to college without penalty of losing course credits.

In July of 2000, Governor Roy Barnes enacted legislation to change the names of technical institutes to technical colleges, and soon

• (above right) Dr. Melton Palmer Jr.—President.

• (right) Admissions personnel are eager to help students select programs that meet their career goals.

thereafter Macon Technical Institute was officially renamed Central Georgia Technical College. The new geographical name was selected to more clearly represent the College's service area.

CGTC offers its students a choice of associate degree programs, diploma programs, and technical certificates of credit as well as a variety of certification options. "We continue to increase our industry certified training programs, so that our business and industry customers can be assured they are employing graduates who will be productive immediately," said college President, Dr. Melton Palmer, Jr., who has served in this capacity since 1989. "The focus of the College has always been to improve services to our customers—whether that includes incorporating ever-changing technological resources to improve the methods in the delivery of quality instruction, or providing an atmosphere where learning takes place in a friendly environment—we're here to ensure the success of our students."

For new and expanding industries, CGTC's Office of Economic Development can provide start-up training or retraining for employees. Another resource available to Georgia businesses is the nationally recognized Quick Start program that is operated by the Department of Technical and Adult Education. The Quick Start program provides high-quality training services at no cost to new or expanding businesses in Georgia. Quick Start has been cited by *Fortune* magazine for its effectiveness in delivering the most comprehensive and advanced training in the nation.

All the accomplishments and milestones that CGTC has achieved have been part of a long-range plan to provide the communities with a skilled, quality workforce. The challenges that face CGTC are similar to those of other higher education institutions. Remaining competitive in a global economy, developing responsive programs to meet the demands of the market, and increasing the partnerships within the community are fundamental to creating a viable workforce. Central Georgia Technical College embraces these challenges each day as part of its mission, its goal, and its philosophy of purpose. ❋

• (above) Students develop a camaraderie that will last a lifetime at CGTC.

• (left) Advisors provide guidance for students and are always available to help.

MOUNT DE SALES ACADEMY

Mount de Sales Academy, home of the Cavaliers, is nestled among the hills and white columns of Macon's downtown historic district where it has served since 1871.

In addition to its downtown campus, Mount de Sales Academy now has an athletic complex, known as Cavalier Fields, located on Interstate Parkway at Columbus Road. The complex, where athletic activities first began taking place in 1998, will also be the site of a Fieldhouse that is currently under construction.

Central Georgia's first academy and only private school to be recognized as a National Blue Ribbon School of Excellence, Mount de Sales has grown from a nationally renowned boarding school for girls to a nationally acclaimed co-educational college preparatory school.

Known for its tradition of academic excellence in a disciplined and caring environment, the academy stands clearly as a Catholic institution aimed at a Gospel-values-oriented way of life. Each student at Mount de Sales is nurtured as a whole person—spiritually, intellectually, socially, and physically, with the ability to make decisions based on beliefs and convictions. Serving students in grades 7 through 12, the academy is exclusively college preparatory. A Mount de Sales Academy education is an investment that pays rich dividends for a lifetime.

• (top) Mount de Sales Academy's Main Building overlooks Macon's downtown historic district.

• (right) Sister Mary Rosina, President of Mount de Sales, visits with students.

Throughout its history, Mount de Sales Academy has consistently emphasized a strong foundation, preparing students for achievement both in college and throughout life. Both honors and advanced placement courses are offered. Mount de Sales students frequently receive both regional and state awards, honors, and academic championships. A high percentage of graduates regularly earn merit scholarships. In 1997, Mount de Sales Academy was honored to receive the Outstanding Catholic Schools for Tomorrow: Excellence in Education award, and again, in 1998, the Academy received the Outstanding Catholic Schools for Tomorrow: Innovations in Technology award.

Fully accredited by the Southern Association of Colleges and Secondary Schools, Mount de Sales Academy is a member of the Georgia Independent Schools Association and operates within the framework of the Catholic Diocese of Savannah. The Academy was founded by the Sisters of Mercy and is now operated by a Board of Trustees. The Sisters of Mercy have a strong tradition of academic excellence in education, and serve in many other worldwide ministries.

Serving as a community of faith as well as a community of learning, Mount de Sales Academy holds the following convictions to be at the heart of the educational endeavor: belief in a personal and loving God, belief in the value of life and dignity of the individual, and belief that each person must be aware of and responsive to obligations of their community. Mount de Sales Academy families appreciate the religious values and lessons that last a lifetime. Frequent schoolwide service activities reinforce the theme that any definition of a successful life must include serving others.

Students at Mount de Sales Academy traditionally have come from varied religious, economic, racial, and ethnic backgrounds. Today, the student community is approximately half Catholic and half other faiths. The academy's ecumenical philosophy has been central to its success. Students develop themselves through a wide variety of extracurricular activities including academic, social, and community activities. Opportunities for leadership and involvement abound. Mount de Sales Academy prepares students for life, with lessons learned on the playing field as well as in the classroom. The competitive athletic program boasts many state championships. Cavaliers have distinguished themselves in both collegiate and professional sports... with the foundation of academics first.

The success of tomorrow begins today. The Mount de Sales Academy graduate joins a proud legacy of alumni. In partnership with student families and other members of the Cavalier family, Mount de Sales Academy continues its role as the area's benchmark in college preparatory education. ❋

• Photo by Ken Krakow

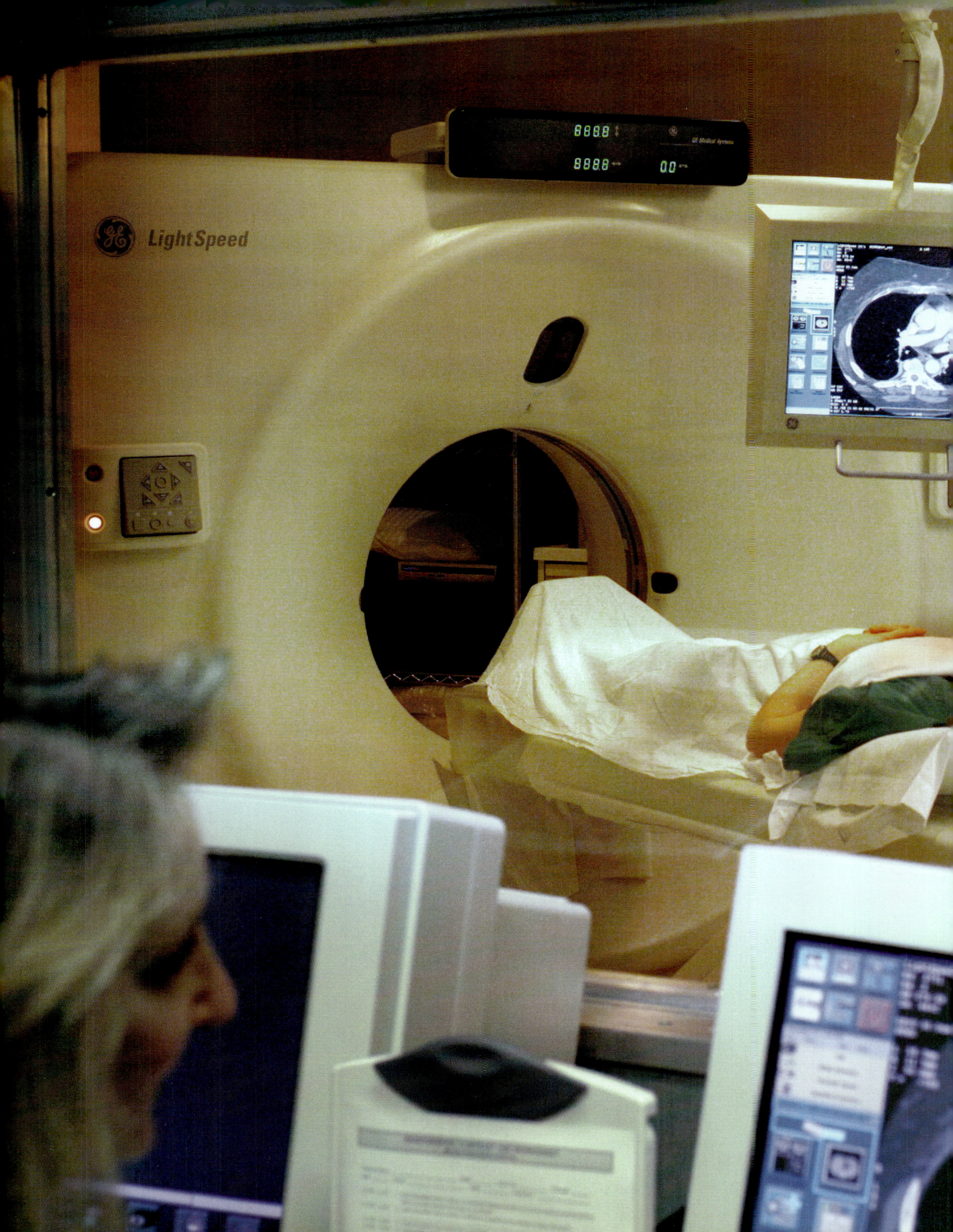
LightSpeed

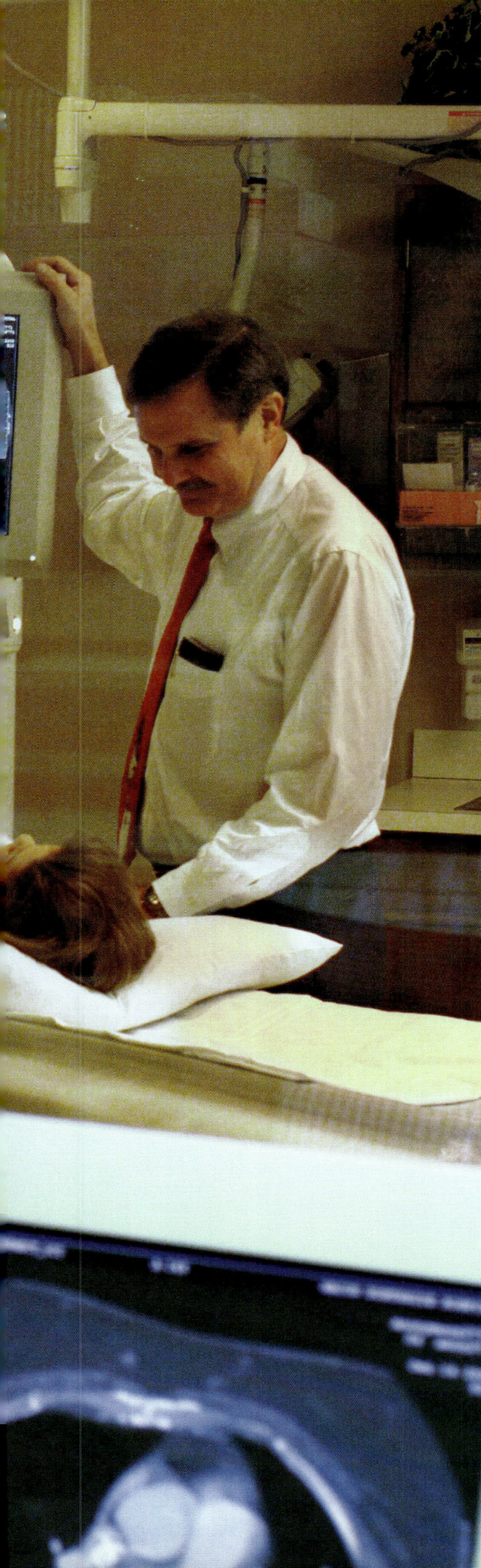

CHAPTER TWELVE

12

Health Care

Photo by Ken Krakow

COLISEUM HEALTH SYSTEM

• (top) Coliseum Medical Centers was founded in 1971 and has established itself as a leader in the medical community with the latest in medical and surgical treatments available.
Photo by Ken Krakow

Health care is an invaluable resource to any community. Middle Georgia is fortunate to have not only many qualified physicians and clinicians but also several top-notch hospital choices. Coliseum Health System is a major player in the medical arena. In May 1998, a joint venture between Columbia/HCA and Quorum, two hospital management companies from Brentwood, Tennessee, formed Coliseum Health System—a three-hospital network comprised of Coliseum Medical Centers, Macon Northside Hospital and Middle Georgia Hospital. Each of these three hospitals creates an important dimension of health care in our area.

COLISEUM MEDICAL CENTERS

Founded in 1971 as Coliseum Park Hospital by Hospital Corporation of America (HCA), Coliseum Medical Centers (a 258-bed facility) has been a leader in medical and surgical services over the last 29 years. The hospital provides a full range of services including inpatient and outpatient medical care, surgery, emergency care, laboratory and radiology services, rehabilitation, and cardiopulmonary care.

In 1973, Coliseum added obstetrics and nursery services and to date over 30,000 babies have started their lives in the Family Ties Birthing Center. The center boasts the title of "Best Place to Have a Baby" as awarded by local readers of *Parenting* magazine. Middle Georgia is also fortunate to have one of the state's neonatal intensive-care units located at Coliseum. This 13-bed unit is specially designed and staffed with neonatal physicians and nurses to treat sick or premature infants.

Since 1984, Coliseum Psychiatric Center has provided high-quality mental-health services to the Middle Georgia area. The Psych Center treats adults and adolescents on an inpatient and outpatient basis for mental-health needs and chemical dependency. They also provide the community with Life-Line, a free mental-health referral and assessment service, which is staffed by trained psychiatric professionals 24 hours a day, 7 days a week.

• (below) Macon's newest hospital, Macon Northside Hospital, opened its doors in 1984. It specializes in the most advanced patient-centered care in a smaller medical environment.

The Coliseum Medical Centers' campus also houses over 50 physician practices in four medical office buildings. With over 80 physicians on the campus representing most major medical specialties, patients find that health care is easily accessible from interstates 75 and 16.

After three years of building renovations, Coliseum now boasts a new exterior, a redesigned, larger emergency room, updated and expanded surgery areas, many relocated hospital departments, and the newest addition to the campus—the Coliseum Surgery and Rehabilitation Center. During the spring of 2000, Coliseum opened this one-of-a-kind center for outpatient surgery, endoscopy, pre-admission testing, and physical, occupational, and recreational therapy patients. All services are provided in one convenient location with easy-to-reach, designated parking.

The Coliseum Breast Health Center is a resource and support service for breast cancer patients and their families.

The center's coordinator is a specially trained oncology nurse who coordinates a patient's care with a multidisciplinary team of physicians and clinicians. The resource library houses the latest literature and videos on breast disease diagnosis and treatment. The Bosom Buddies Support Group meets twice monthly for patients who find benefit in the emotional strength of the group. The Coliseum Women's Center is located just steps away from the Breast Health Center to give patients immediate attention. The Women's Center is an outpatient diagnostic center for women, providing outpatient mammography, bone densitometry, ultrasound, and other radiology services in one convenient location.

The Metabolic Center is a treatment center for patients with diabetes, lipid disorders, osteoporosis, thyroid disease, and stroke effects. Monthly classes and support groups are available to patients as well as individual sessions with the center's dietician and registered nurse. Patients also have the option of participating in unique educational activities such as the "Healthy Eating Super Market Tours" or regularly scheduled free screenings. Also, Stroke Recovery Services are offered to patients and families through the Metabolic Center. The center provides education and the Strive from Stroke Support Group to interested patients.

Coliseum Rehabilitation Center is an inpatient and outpatient rehab hospital located at Coliseum Medical Centers. The inpatient center, located on the fourth floor of the hospital, is self-sufficient with its own cafeteria, gymnasium, and transitional living apartment. Patients recovering from orthopedic surgery, strokes, or major injuries come to the Rehab Center for physical, occupational, speech, and recreational therapy. It is the goal of the therapists to help patients and families learn how to adjust back to a normal lifestyle or altered daily routine.

MACON NORTHSIDE HOSPITAL

Macon's newest hospital, Macon Northside Hospital, was built in 1984 by the Charter Medical Corporation as Charter Northside Hospital. Nestled among the Georgia pines in North Macon, this 103-bed, neighborhood hospital provides sophisticated inpatient and outpatient medical, surgical emergency, laboratory, radiology, and rehabilitation services.

The newest arrival at Macon Northside is the Baby Garden Birth Center, which opened in October of 1997. This one-of-a-kind, garden-theme birth center provides families a peaceful, private setting where physicians and nurses focus on individual family needs. The Baby Garden surprises patients with special amenities such as hand-painted garden murals, soothing classical music, afternoon tea time, an annual garden birthday party, and prenatal classes to suit patients' educational needs.

The 24-hour emergency room is conveniently located close to many residential, shopping, and school areas. Also, the emergency physicians and staff are trained to treat major to minor illnesses, with a chest pain clinic available for possible cardiac patients. On the campus, four medical office buildings house 36 physician practices representing 16 medical specialties.

MIDDLE GEORGIA HOSPITAL

Located in the heart of historic Macon, Middle Georgia Hospital has provided a tradition of quality service since 1911. Originally founded as Williams Private Sanatorium, Middle Georgia's commitment to quality has remained the same and now it stands as a full service medical-surgical hospital with 119 beds, over 300 employees, and 106 active physicians on staff. Patients receive quality medical and surgical inpatient and outpatient services including laboratory, radiology, cardiopulmonary, and rehabilitation.

Middle Georgia Hospital was the first hospital in Macon to perform diagnostic testing with specialized heart catheterization equipment. The hospital's outpatient services allow patients to

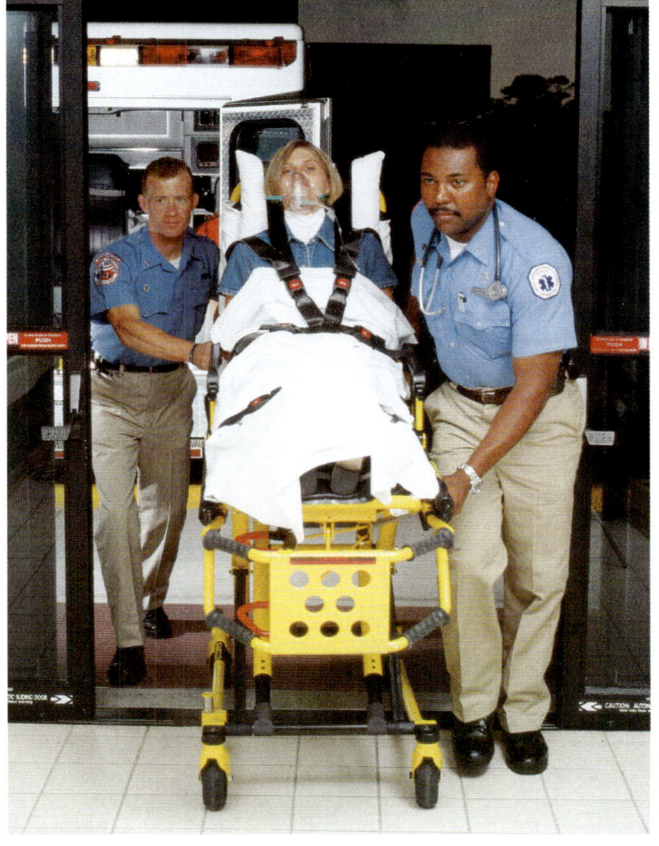

• (top) Middle Georgia Hospital was founded in 1911 as Williams Sanitorium. The hospital provides the community with unique medical services such as the Wound Healing and Hyperbaric Medicine Center and the Senior Center, a geriatric psychiatric unit for patients 65 years and older.

• (left) With two emergency rooms located on opposite sides of town, the community has easy access to emergency care regardless of where they live, work, or play.

undergo tests and procedures without having to spend the night, and the Surgery Today, Home Today wing offers private rooms.

Patients suffering from chronic non-healing wounds are fortunate to have the Wound Healing and Hyperbaric Medicine Center of Middle Georgia Hospital. The center provides a multidisciplinary approach to wound management using the specialized skills of a team of experienced physicians, nurses, and therapists. This team works together to design innovative treatment programs that are individualized in an effort to promote the quickest and fullest possible recovery. The Wound Healing Center manages any wound present more than 30 days or wounds failing to improve with multiple treatments or therapies including diabetic foot ulcers, pressure ulcers, failing skin grafts, and late effect of radiation treatment. Together with patients and their doctors, the center offers promise for wounds that are difficult to heal.

Middle Georgia Hospital's centralized location downtown is within yards of the majority of medical office buildings in Macon. Physicians and their patients have easy access to a hospital with a longstanding reputation for outstanding medical care.

SENIOR SERVICES

Middle Georgia's growing senior population is well taken care of with Coliseum Health System, and services are available to meet medical, educational, social, and psychological needs. For medical care, the Senior Health Center, a primary-care physician practice, exclusively treats patients ages 65 and older. Located at Coliseum Medical Centers in Building C, the center is staffed with a registered nurse and outreach coordinator trained to care for and refer seniors to appropriate local resources. They host monthly screenings and seminars with the physician to discuss topics relevant to seniors such as high blood pressure, diabetes, and heart disease.

Also, the Senior Center at Middle Georgia Hospital is a geriatric psychiatric unit specially designed to diagnose and treat mental illness in people over 65 years of age. Many families do not realize there is a normal and abnormal aging process. This 16-bed unit is specifically for patients with abnormal aging, depression, Alzheimer's Disease, or other mental illness.

Next, Middle Georgia is fortunate to have a local chapter of the national organization, Senior Friends. Senior Friends is the second largest seniors' organization next to AARP and the local chapter has over 1,000 members. In a partnership with Wesleyan College, the Senior Friends office is located on Tucker Road on the school's beautiful campus. This gives members access to large meeting facilities

• (top) Each year, thousands of families welcome their new arrivals with the assistance of the Family Ties Birthing Center at Coliseum Medical Centers and the Baby Garden Birth Center at Macon Northside Hospital.

• (right) In the spring of 2000, the Coliseum Surgery and Rehabilitation Center opened as the first freestanding full-service ambulatory care center in Middle Georgia.

as well as a brand-new, state-of-the-art fitness center. Senior Friends members enjoy benefits and activities such as monthly meetings and seminars, exercise classes, in-town and out-of-town trips, weekly card games, and discounts on services like car rentals, prescriptions, travel, etc.

Seniors play a vital role in the hospitals' volunteer programs. Although volunteers range in age from 14 to 88, it is the seniors who devote so much precious time to the hospital patients and families. From clerical duties in hospital departments to delivering patient mail, to keeping the literature current in waiting rooms, these volunteers provide an invaluable service to everyone. At Macon Northside Hospital, the volunteers even own and manage the hospital gift shop. Money is raised through the gift shop, and other fundraising events, such as the annual jewelry sales, to support scholarships for Bibb County high school seniors entering a health-care related field. To date, over $10,000 in scholarships have been awarded to local students. The volunteers at Coliseum Medical Centers host annual book sales to raise money for local community non-profit organizations.

Last, there are many programs affiliated with Coliseum Health System which are not solely for seniors but which cater to their needs. For example, the Metabolic Center, Stroke Recovery Services, Breast Health Center, Wound Healing Center, and Rehabilitation Center all provide seniors with much needed community resources and services.

All of the hospitals affiliated with Coliseum Health System have always been committed to serving this community with quality, affordable health care in a setting that is best for the patient and physician. As the new millennium begins, this commitment will not change. Like all forms of technology, medicine and available treatments are improving and advancing at a rapid speed.

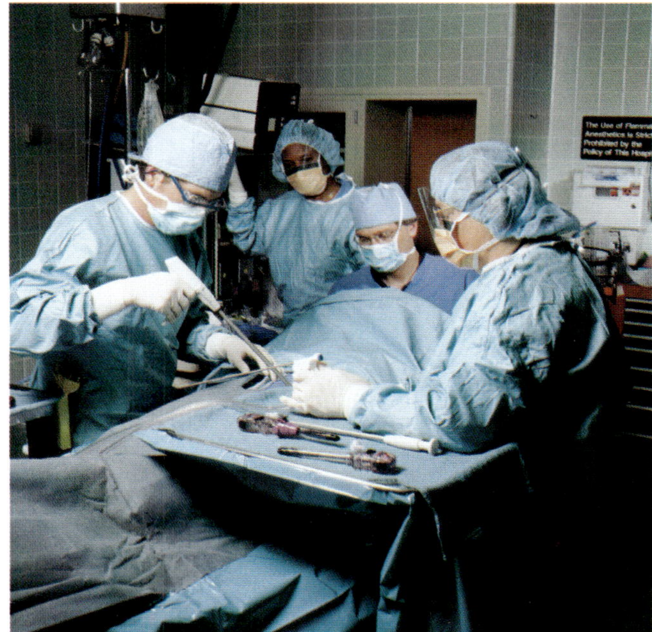

These hospitals will continue to remain at the helm of this technological wave while keeping patients and their personal needs for service and individual care foremost in mind.

In the future, patients should expect to see more surgical procedures that are less invasive and require less recovery time. Treatments will be available for illnesses and diseases that were thought to be incurable or inoperable. Vaccinations may even be available for certain forms of cancer. But, regardless of the sophisticated world of technology and medical research, Coliseum Health System hospitals and employees will remain at the forefront of the most important aspect of health care—the personal, caring touch. ❋

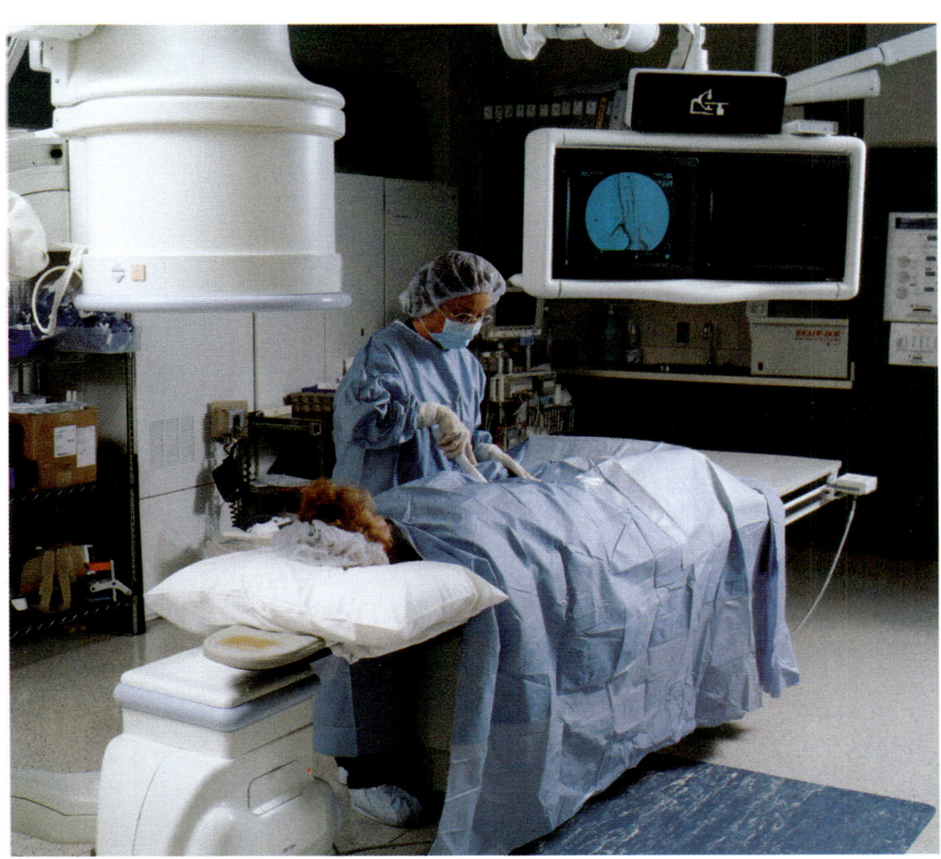

• (top) Cutting-edge surgery is performed at all three Coliseum Health Systems hospitals.

• (left) Middle Georgians have the latest diagnostic procedures available to them through Coliseum Medical Centers, Macon Northside Hospital, and Middle Georgia Hospital.

CENTRAL GEORGIA HEALTH SYSTEM

Central Georgia Health System: Beyond All Barriers

About five years ago a beautiful "coffee table book" was published called *A HOSPITAL WITHOUT WALLS: The First 100 Years of The Medical Center of Central Georgia*. Its bold illustrations and behind the scenes revelations about development of this Macon institution told the story of The Med from creation to the then present. The title however, means even more today with the creation of Central Georgia Health System (CGHS). Through CGHS, not only has the barrier of walls been torn down, but geographic boundaries as well.

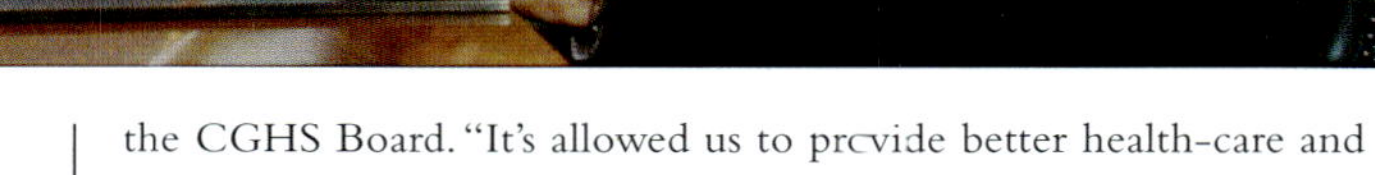

Why a "system?" Don Faulk, president and CEO of CGHS and The Medical Center of Central Georgia (MCCG) explains. "Operating a hospital only inhibited our financial structure, and we believed we needed to remove artificial barriers to health care in this region and, in effect, hardwire regional relationships," he says. In other words, instead of waiting for those in need to come to a building in Macon, board and hospital leadership wanted to bring health care to where people lived.

"We have the largest health-care facility in the region," Faulk says. "We have a responsibility to see our neighbors have access to the best care we can provide." This is done through a system which serves as a parent company over several entities, which include The Medical Center of Central Georgia, Central Georgia Senior Health, Medcen Community Health Foundation, Central Georgia Health Ventures, Centra Management Services, Health Services of Central Georgia, Central Georgia Ancillary Health Systems, Georgia Healthcare Linen Services, and Central Georgia Home Care Services. "To compete with for-profit health-care institutions and offer a wholistic approach to serving the community instead of just one facility, we had to create a system," says Bill Odom, chairman of the CGHS Board. "It's allowed us to provide better health-care and still keep costs down."

Larry Parks is president of Health Services of Central Georgia (HSCG), one of these entities. "We have primary-care physicians located in 10 counties but there's another 10 we would like to add to our placements," he says. "As managed-care programs increase in popularity, our relationships with these physicians will provide much needed additional support for them to serve their patients." He admits it's a challenge. "We're putting physicians in communities that do not represent a financial attraction to most professionals, but through HSCG, we try to make it work for them Then they are there to work for you." Through CGHS, walls truly are being torn down.

• (top right) A. Donald Faulk, Jr., FACHE President/CEO.

• (below) Central Georgia Health System Board, from left: First row, seated: William W. Orr, Don Faulk, Bill Odom, Barbara Clowers. Second row: Peter Solomon, William Hutchings, Deitz Carpenter, Billy Jackson. Not pictured: Steve Kruger, Andy Galloway.

The Medical Center of Central Georgia: A Beacon of Hope

It looms on the Macon skyline, truly a city landmark. The largest plant employer in Bibb County with a red beacon in the night that reads The Medical Center. But as massive as the "brick and mortar" is, The Medical Center of Central Georgia (MCCG) is so much more.

When asked what he is most proud of about MCCG, Don Faulk, president and CEO didn't hesitate. "It's the people who have transformed this facility into a world-class institution," he says. "There is a lot of money pumped into a lot of medical facilities, but money alone won't make you good. At MCCG, there is a spirit... a spirit of compassion and caring that permeates all we do, and that makes all the difference."

Most Macon area residents have experienced this spirit at one time or another. Others just sense they can rely on it if the time comes. Peter Solomon, president/CEO of Coldwell Banker/SSK Realtors and chairman of the MCCG Board, says, "MCCG is a primary benefit of relocations to this area. We can point to it with tremendous pride."

Faulk remembers when this wasn't always so. But, as commitments were made and met,

as support was sought and given, MCCG became the health core of the community. "Make no mistake, the people in the community had to adopt us as we improved, but the more they trusted us, the more we improved and the more the word got out. The community is as much a part of our success story as anything else."

Another part is well known by Barb Stickel, a senior vice president. "Don is right about our employees making the difference, but this kind of support doesn't happen by chance," she says. "We are very selective in our employment standards. Once employed, we are determined to advance employees' knowledge with seminars, workshops, and work experience that helps them grow. And perhaps even more important, we listen to employees. The receptionist who heard a family member ask about some service or consideration, can tell us how to improve our service. Listening to employees and sharing ideas at all levels is how we constantly get better."

As Mike Gilstrap, executive vice president/COO of MCCG considers the future of this institution, he sees how some things may change, and some will not. "It's the nature of health care that inside the brick and mortar there will be a greater focus on critical intensive care," he predicts. "But the true impact of MCCG will actually grow as its impact spreads out into the communities around us." You might say it will always be the nucleus of health care in this region, but from it the spirit will spread far beyond the red beacon atop the building downtown.

The Children's Hospital at The Medical Center of Georgia: Making a Difference

"Children are not little adults." That quote could be attributed to everyone who works in The Children's Hospital at The Medical Center of Central Georgia (MCCG) because it is a mantra that goes to the core of the difference in health care for children.

Nowhere is that mantra pursued more doggedly than at The Children's Hospital. What began as a six-bed unit has grown to a substantial section of the third floor of MCCG. The Children's Hospital has developed a web of services that spreads out to embrace the needs of these special patients.

"We have crystallized an entire health-care system for children right here in Macon," says Dr. Frank Bowyer, medical director of The Children's Hospital. "It starts with pediatric specialists in every specialty. They educate those around them. Meanwhile, MCCG has invested in equipment and people to operate not just a Neonatal Intensive Care Unit (NICU), but a Pediatric Intensive Care Unit (PICU) as well."

• (top) Peyton Anderson Health Education Center dedicated April 2000.

• (left) Medical Center of Central Georgia Board, from left: First row, seated: Don Faulk, Bill Odom, Peter Solomon, Alan Kirsh, Albert Abrams.
Second row: Mike Gilstrap, Damon King, Barbara Clowers, Ellis Evans, Jerry Payne, Louise Bryant, John Comer, Shirley Irvin.
Third row: Sturla Stefansson, Emory Johnson, Billy Jackson.

Bowyer says a team management approach is used to cover all the bases. PICU addresses trauma, NICU addresses newborn care, a special cancer center for children provides necessary treatment, and he is recruiting a pediatric neurology specialist to coordinate the work of pediatric neurosurgeons, pediatric orthopedists, and pediatric behavior specialists.

With children, there's more to treatment than medicine, and Dawn Cole nursing director, says the Hospital's Child Life Support Team makes all the difference. "These people are talented professionals with one mission—helping children emotionally get through their treatment," she says. They talk with frightened children and distract children waiting for procedures. "They are part of the team with the doctors, nurses, and other support staff," she says.

In a way, the presence of The Medical Center of Central Georgia in the region may be best known through The Children's Hospital. "Our PICU really serves the entire children's population in this region," says Barb Stickel, "because once a diagnosis has been made in the PICU and the necessary treatment initiated, it can often be continued by the pediatrician in that child's community." Having that kind of care in these rural communities sends out a special message.

"Childcare strikes an emotional chord in the community," says Don Faulk. "It's my hope as time passes and our outreach efforts with children grow, there will be a preventative quality to our efforts and a steadily declining need for this precious population to require hospital treatment at all." Now that would truly make a difference to this very different kind of patient.

The Georgia Heart Center: A Finger on the Pulse

The Georgia Heart Center at The Medical Center of Central Georgia is once again leading the way in providing the best in heart care by becoming the only hospital in Central Georgia to provide beating heart bypass surgery as an option for patients with coronary artery disease.

Until recently, simple bypass surgery usually meant stopping the heart from beating during surgery and rerouting blood flow through a heart lung machine. Now, thanks to The Medtronic Octopus®2+ Tissue Stabilization System now being used at The Medical Center, surgeons can stabilize a portion of the heart while they suture—eliminating the need to stop the patient's heart. This means patients may enjoy shorter hospital stays and recovery times than with traditional bypass surgery.

This is just one of the many reasons why renowned Health Care Information Association has ranked it as one of the top 100 hospitals in the nation for cardiac intervention. On a local level or on a national level, MCCG's Georgia Heart Center is the place to go for cardiac care.

"It's simply a natural evolution of our population as people live longer that cardiac care is increasingly needed. Just as the need for this care grows, so does the need to improve treatment," says Don Faulk. "For us, it all intersects here. We've consolidated our cardiac care services for maximum effectiveness."

As a private practice cardiologist Dr. John Hawkins has been working at MCCG for 18 years and performs approximately 1,500 procedures a year. "Yes, this is a high-volume facility for cardiac care, and that's part of the advantage here," he says. "I come in here knowing I'll be working with a support staff that knows these procedures as well as I do. I can rely on them, and that really reduces complications."

Dr. Carl Lane is chief of the medical staff and a cardiovascular surgeon at The Heart Center. "Technology has made it possible for us to conduct operations on high-risk patients that just would not have been candidates for surgery a few years ago," he says. "Even so, we conduct a careful screening process to evaluate less invasive treatments whenever possible. It's encouraging to see we have surgical options today that didn't exist before. We can save more lives." ❋

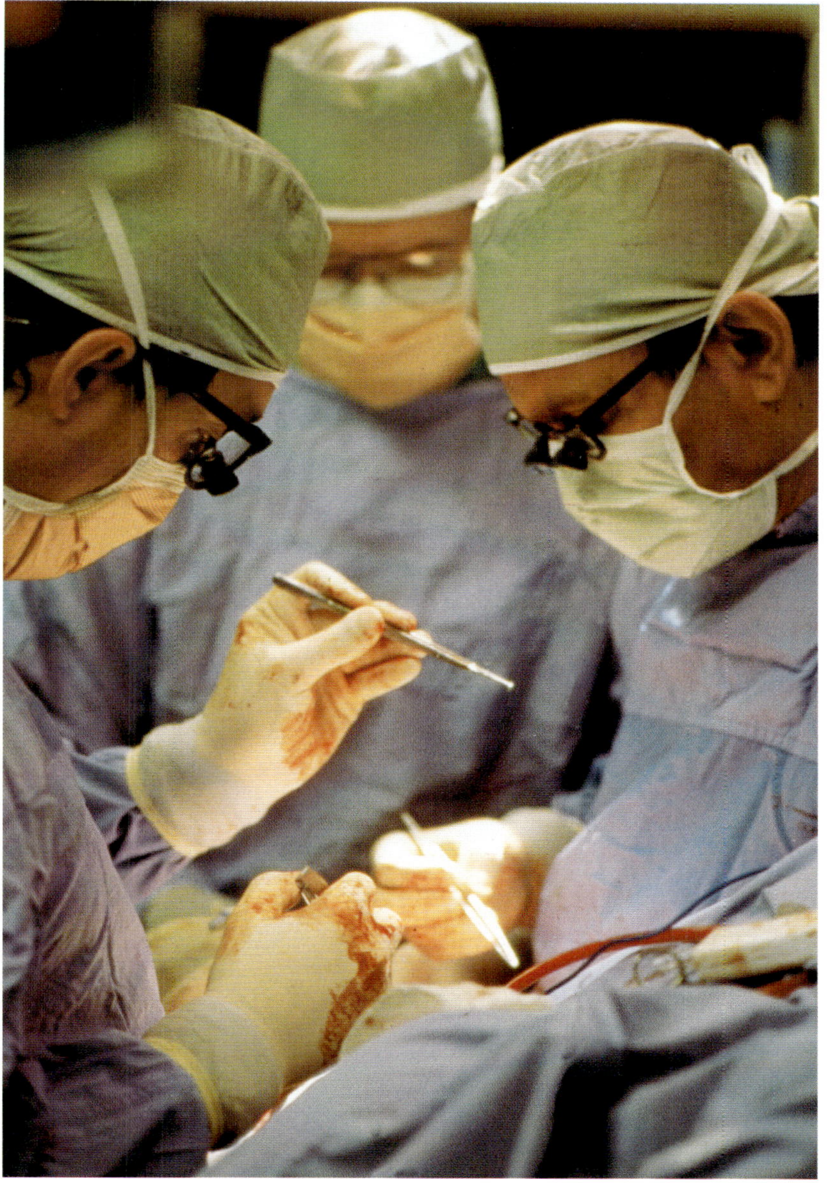

• (top) Georgia's third most active heart program in 1999.

• (left) Heartworks Rehabilitation.

FORSYTH STREET ORTHOPAEDIC SURGERY & REHABILITATION CENTER

When members of the Macon Braves minor-league baseball team take a tumble on the playing field, they head to Forsyth Street Orthopaedic Surgery and Rehabilitation Center for help in recovering from their sports-related injuries.

Athletes with the city's popular Sally League team aren't the only ones who can benefit from the center's staff of highly trained doctors, physical and occupational therapists, and certified athletic trainers. The center's specialists also stand ready to provide advanced, effective, and comprehensive care for sufferers of all types of orthopaedic injuries, athletic and non-athletic alike. Regardless of age or the origin of orthopaedic injuries, the center has complete facilities and expertise for treatment.

Located at 1600 Forsyth Street, the approximately 26,000-square-foot, state-of-the-art complex boasts examining rooms, x-ray equipment, plaster rooms, hydrotherapy facilities, and a gym complete with equipment for therapy, evaluation, and exercise.

Since Dr. Frank B. Kelly and Dr. Charles H. Richardson founded the center in 1980, it has grown to include three other partners. In 1987, Dr. Gary L. Hattaway joined the practice, and in 1989, the three doctors and their rehabilitation team moved into their new facility on Forsyth Street. Joining the practice in 1993, Dr. Joseph E. Slappey became a partner the following year. Dr. Timothy R. Stapleton joined the team in 1997 and became a partner on January 1, 2000.

The center's five orthopaedic surgeons offer specialized treatment in total joint replacement, spinal disorders, arthroscopic surgery, and shoulder reconstruction. Their philosophy of orthopaedic treatment and rehabilitation is simple: to provide their patients suffering from orthopedic injuries the most advanced, effective, and comprehensive treatment available, thereby ensuring patients a complete recovery and quick return to their active lifestyles. Diversity in training allows the center's specialists to treat a full range of orthopaedic injuries, and each of the doctors brings a particular area of expertise to the medical practice.

Dr. Kelly, a Phi Beta Kappa graduate of the University of North Carolina at Chapel Hill, completed his medical training at the Medical College of Georgia and served his orthopaedic surgery residency at the University of Tennessee. Board-certified by the American Board of Orthopaedic Society, Dr. Kelly also teaches at Mercer Medical School. He specializes in joint replacement and arthroscopic surgery and speaks around the world to other doctors on total joint replacements.

A graduate of Vanderbilt University, Dr. Richardson earned his medical degree from the Medical College of Georgia in August and completed his orthopaedic surgery training at The Johns Hopkins Hospital in Baltimore, Maryland. A faculty member of Mercer Medical School, he is board-certified by the American Board of Orthopaedic Surgery and specializes in the treatment of spinal disorders and problems of the lower extremities.

Dr. Hattaway, a graduate of Emory University in Atlanta, earned his medical degree with honors from the Medical College of Georgia in Augusta. Board-certified by the American Board of Orthopaedic Surgery and a member of AOA Medical Honor Society, he completed his orthopaedic surgery training at Georgia

• (above) Located at 1600 Forsyth Street, the complex offers passersby an impressive sight, with its jutting front columns and rows of glistening glass.

• (right) The center's five orthopaedic surgeons, from left: Timothy R. Stapleton, M.D.; Frank B. Kelly, M.D. (seated); Charles H. Richardson, M.D.; Gary L. Hattaway, M.D.; Joseph E. Slappey Jr., M.D. Photos by Ken Krakow

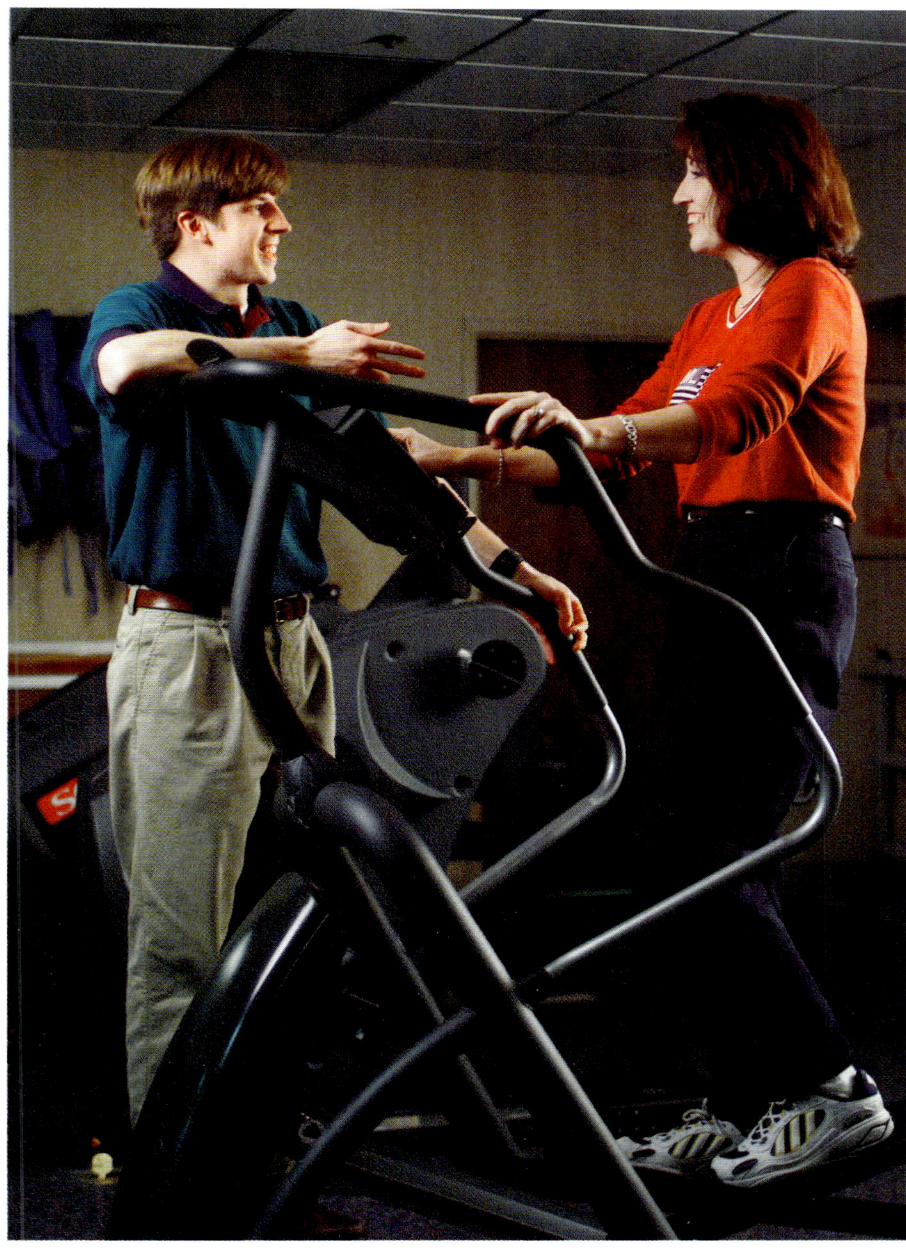

• (left) The center's specialists stand ready to provide advanced, effective, and comprehensive care for sufferers of all types of orthopaedic injuries. Photo by Ken Krakow

Baptist Medical Center and specializes in joint replacement, arthroscopic surgery, and spine surgery.

Dr. Slappey graduated from Georgia Southwestern College and received his medical degree from the Medical College of Georgia. He completed a six-year residency and one-year internship at Georgia Baptist Medical Center in Atlanta. Specializing in general orthopaedics, he is board-certified by the American Board of Orthopaedic Surgery.

Dr. Stapleton graduated magna cum laude from Mercer University, earned his medical degree at Mercer Medical School, and completed his orthopaedic surgery residency in San Antonio while in the Air Force. Board-certified by the American Board of Orthopaedic Surgery and Assistant Clinical Professor at Mercer Medical School, he specializes in sports medicine, shoulder reconstruction, and joint replacement.

Tommy Williamson, P.T., was named medical director of the center's rehabilitation department in 1990. The rehabilitation team consists of six physical therapists and certified athletic trainers.

Forsyth Street Orthopaedic Surgery & Rehabilitation Center now has an assembled corps of over 50 employees in the physicians' and therapists' offices. In addition to serving as team physicians for the Macon Braves, the doctors at the center perform similar services for Mercer University, as well as several area private schools. The center—the first of its kind in Middle Georgia—features a convenient location near Interstate 75 and Interstate 16, affording easy accessibility to patients in Macon and throughout the Middle Georgia area.

The doctors on staff at Forsyth Street Orthopaedic Surgery & Rehabilitation Center are affiliated with all local hospitals. Their Web site—www.forsythstreetortho.com—provides educational information for their patients, as well as for other consumers. ❋

• (below) Seated from left, Forsyth Street Orthopaedics founders: Frank B. Kelly, M.D. and Charles H. Richardson, M.D., with Manager Pam Folsom and Director of Physical Therapy Tommy Williamson.

THE MACON ORTHOPAEDIC AND HAND CENTER

The physicians and staff at The Macon Orthopaedic and Hand Center care about what they do. Letters and success stories adorn the hallways and walls of the doctors' offices. Smiles and friendly greetings welcome patients as they enter the waiting room, and shelves of literature and medical information are at your fingertips, as the doctors and staff know that an informed patient is always the best patient.

It all began with Dr. Waldo Floyd, Jr. Born and raised in South Georgia, Dr. Floyd followed in the footsteps of his father, and numerous others in the family tree, in becoming a doctor.

After receiving his medical degree from The Johns Hopkins Medical School in Baltimore, Maryland, Dr. Floyd completed advanced training at Grady Memorial Hospital, Georgia Baptist Hospital, and hospitals at The Medical College of Georgia. In 1961, he settled in Macon and founded the practice.

Word of Dr. Floyd's compassion and skill as a physician quickly spread throughout Georgia as he pioneered the development of orthopaedic surgery in the region. Dr. Floyd was among the first surgeons in the state to perform total joint replacement, and he gained widespread recognition for his work in reconstructive hand surgery. The growing practice led to the addition of another skilled Georgia physician, Dr. Alexander H. S. Weaver, Jr.

Dr. Weaver joined Dr. Floyd in 1967 after graduating from Mercer University and receiving his doctorate at The Medical College of Georgia, where he also completed his orthopaedic training. He was an Orthopaedic Surgery Instructor at Talmadge Memorial Hospital in Augusta, Georgia, before serving in the United States Army for two years at Martin Army Hospital, Fort Benning, where he was Chief of Orthopaedic Surgery. Dr. Weaver continued on staff at The Macon Orthopaedic and Hand Center until he passed away in October of 1999.

The practice continued to grow and flourish as patients came, not only from Macon, but throughout the state as well. In 1974, native Maconite, C. Emory Johnson, Jr., joined the staff after finishing his undergraduate education at Emory University and receiving his medical degree at The Medical College of Georgia. He trained in orthopaedic surgery at both Georgia Baptist Hospital and the Scottish Rite Children's Hospital in Atlanta. He returned to Macon after a two-year stint in the United States Air Force where he served as the Chief of Orthopaedic Surgery at Shaw Air Force Base in Sumter, South Carolina.

The three doctors were busy, with Dr. Floyd specializing in reconstructive hand and upper extremity surgery, and Drs. Weaver and Johnson specializing in general orthopaedic surgery with a special interest in foot and ankle disorders, arthroscopy, joint replacement, and children's orthopaedic problems.

In 1987, The Macon Orthopaedic and Hand Center proudly opened its arms to another doctor. Dr. Waldo Floyd, III, joined his father and Drs. Weaver and Johnson. Dr. Floyd, III, received his medical degree from Emory University and further training in surgery at The Johns Hopkins Hospital. He completed his residency in orthopaedic surgery at Harvard Medical School where he was Chief Resident at the Massachusetts General Hospital and completed a fellowship in hand surgery at Roosevelt Hospital in New York City.

Dr. Floyd, III, specializes in surgery of the hand and upper limb. He was among the first micro-hand surgeons in the region and has received widespread recognition. He has published numerous articles and book chapters dealing with hand and orthopaedic surgery. He is a Clinical Assistant Professor of Orthopaedic Surgery at Emory University School of Medicine and a Clinical Professor of Surgery at Mercer University School of Medicine.

The doctors were working continuously as their reputation continued to spread across the state. In 1992, Dr. John Sapp joined the team after graduating from The Medical College of Georgia and completing a residency in plastic surgery at Louisiana State University in New Orleans. After spending an additional year at the University of Florida as a fellow in hand and microsurgery, he came to Macon and now specializes in hand surgery and microsurgery—the transfer of tissue from one area of the body to another and replantation following amputations—as well as arthroscopy of the wrist.

In addition to memberships in professional medical organizations, Dr. Sapp is also on the

• (top) Pictured from left: Back row: Dr. C. Emory Johnson, Dr. John W. Sapp, Dr. Michael L. Beckish. Front row: Dr. Waldo E. Floyd, Jr., Dr. Robert M. Thornsberry, Dr. Guy D. Foulkes, and Dr. Waldo E. Floyd, III.

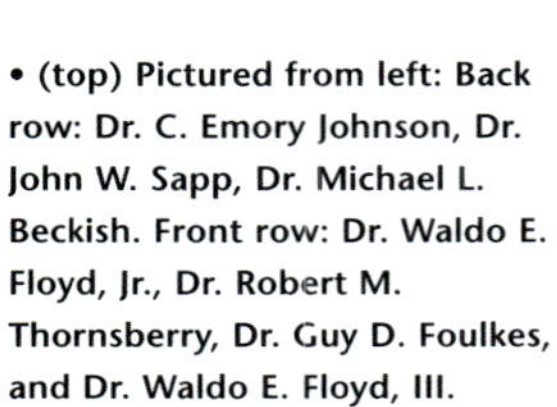

• (right) Dr. Waldo E. Floyd, Jr., seated, and Dr. Waldo E. Floyd, III. Photos by Ken Krakow

faculty of Mercer University School of Medicine as Clinical Assistant Professor in the Department of Surgery.

The Macon Orthopaedic and Hand Center sees approximately 25,000 patients yearly and is still growing. To continue to be able to care for the medical needs of the people of Georgia, the practice has welcomed three new doctors to its staff since the summer of 1995.

Native Georgian, Dr. Robert Thornsberry, attended Davidson College and The Medical College of Georgia. He completed his residency in orthopaedic surgery at the University of Kentucky College of Medicine and completed his fellowship in sports injuries and total joint replacement to complement and expand the work that was already being performed by the practice's other doctors. Dr. Thornsberry has developed an outstanding reputation as a conscientious and effective orthopaedic surgeon.

Shortly after Dr. Thornsberry's arrival, Dr. Guy Foulkes joined the staff. A graduate of Mercer University School of Medicine, he did his internship in general surgery at The Medical Center here in Macon. He completed his orthopaedic residency at the University of Hawaii, and completed his fellowship in hand surgery at UCLA. An accomplished writer, he has published and presented numerous papers on orthopaedic surgery, specifically hand surgery. Through his expertise in hand surgery, Dr. Foulkes has further strengthened the center's ability to care for patients with hand and upper extremity affliction.

In September of 1999, Dr. Michael Beckish, a pediatric orthopaedic surgeon, joined the staff at The Macon Orthopaedic and Hand Center. Dr. Beckish received his undergraduate degree from The Pennsylvania State University. After earning his medical degree from the University of Minnesota, he completed his residency in orthopaedic surgery at Duke University and then spent an additional year as a fellow in pediatric orthopaedic surgery at the University of Utah. He has a special interest in orthopaedic anomalies, including cerebral palsy, clubfoot, and scoliosis. He is trained in limb lengthening and hip reconstruction.

The physicians at The Macon Orthopaedic and Hand Center opened their own outpatient surgery center in February of 1999. Macon Outpatient Surgery, Inc. is located in the same building as the practice at 840 Pine Street in downtown Macon. This state-of-the-art, freestanding, twin-operating-suite facility was opened to provide outpatient surgical care for their patients.

The logo for The Macon Orthopaedic and Hand Center is the symbol for orthopaedics—that of a bent tree being supported and straightened—and since Dr. Floyd Jr.'s humble beginning in 1961, Macon Orthopaedic has been supporting the people of Middle Georgia.

When Dr. Floyd, III, was asked why he thought the practice his father started almost 40 years ago was so successful, he smiled and quietly answered, "The bottom line is, the gentleman who founded this practice cares a lot about people."

That statement is evident today and it applies to each doctor, nurse, x-ray technician, and the entire staff—The Macon Orthopaedic and Hand Center cares about people. ❋

• (top) Dr. Michael L. Beckish, Dr. Guy D. Foulkes, and Dr. C. Emory Johnson peruse a patient's x-ray.

• (left) Dr. John W. Sapp, Dr. Waldo E. Floyd, III, and Dr. Robert M. Thornsberry.
Photos by Ken Krakow

PIEDMONT ORTHOPAEDIC AND SPORTS MEDICINE

Piedmont Orthopaedic and Sports Medicine Complex's team of specialists is committed to giving patients the highest quality of orthopaedic care available. Providing a clinic, surgical center, athletic surgery and rehabilitation, as well as occupational medicine, the Piedmont team is comprised of orthopaedic surgeons, occupational medicine specialists, a physician assistant, registered nurses, licensed and certified athletic trainers, physical therapists, and the clinical staff. The entire team here wants to make all visits to Piedmont as pleasant as possible.

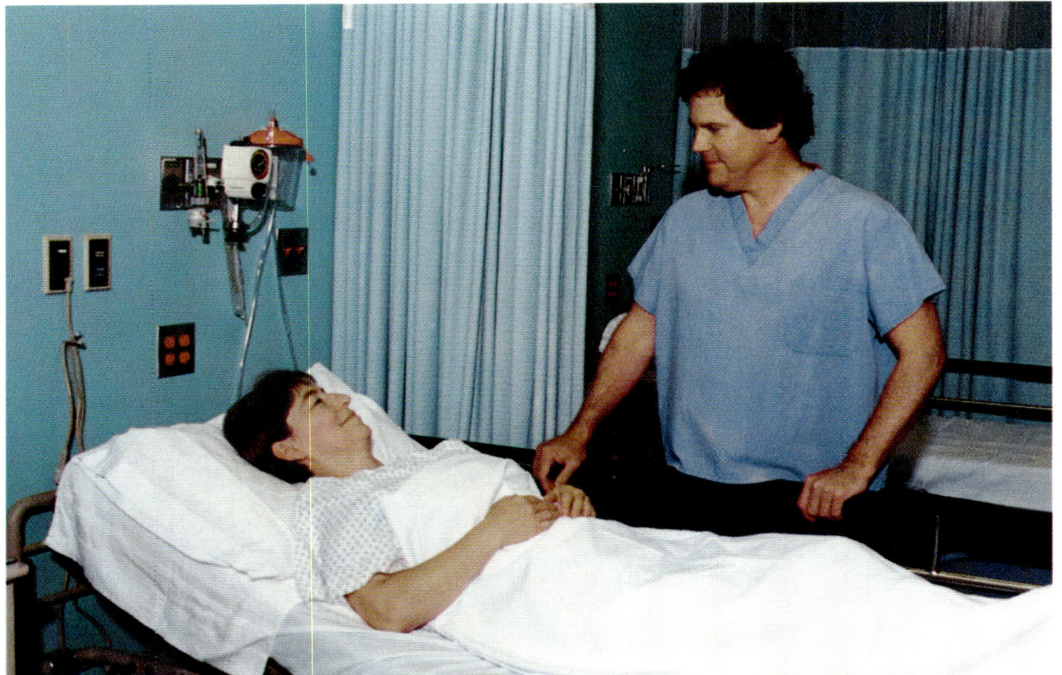

Piedmont Orthopaedic and Sports Medicine Complex's modern, approximately 40,000-square-foot complex is located on a beautiful 20-acre campus at 4660 Riverside Park Boulevard off Riverside Drive near I-75. Piedmont was founded by the late Dr. Walter P. Barnes Jr. and his sons, Dr. Stephen N. Barnes and Dr. William S. Barnes, who put together clinical, surgical, rehabilitative, and occupational medicine services in one organization. The complex in Macon houses the surgeons' offices, surgery center, and rehabilitation and occupational medicine; a satellite office in Warner Robins offers occupational medicine and rehabilitative services.

At Piedmont, effective treatment starts with diagnosis. The complex combines the highly skilled people and state-of-the-art equipment to help get patients back in action. Piedmont's services include everything from children's orthopaedics to delicate hand surgery, from aggressive sports medicine to total joint replacements, from spinal surgery and management to foot and ankle treatment. Piedmont's services even include innovative injury prevention programs and job site analysis and pre-employment screenings. Its physicians and staff are here to serve with total personalized care—from diagnosis to treatment to rehabilitation.

Piedmont's on-site ambulatory surgery center allows doctors to keep a close eye on their patients after surgery. The surgery center boasts two-surgical suites and state-of-the-art equipment and the latest technologies. Its professional staff is devoted to providing every comfort for its patients' stays and to ensuring that they receive the highest-quality care available—while controlling costs.

The surgery center is outpatient or same-day surgery only. Numerous outpatient surgeries now offered include arthroscopy, open rotator cuff repair, and carpal tunnel repair. After these procedures, the patient is able to recuperate in the comfort of his or her own home, but one of the physicians is always on call. The physicians at Piedmont, however, also have surgical privileges at Macon Northside Hospital, Coliseum Park Hospital, and Middle Georgia Hospital. Piedmont also has an association with Dr. Bob Bruce with Emory University in Atlanta for pediatric orthopaedics.

With a major emphasis on sports medicine, Piedmont Orthopaedic and Sports Medicine Complex offers the following: team coverage—attendance by physicians and certified, licensed athletic trainers at high school, college, city, and county athletic events; and required pre-participation physicals for high school and college athletes. It is also a clinical training facility for medical students, medical assistants, x-ray technicians, athletic trainers, and physical therapists.

Dr. Stephen N. Barnes graduated from Virginia Polytechnical Institute and received a doctorate in medicine and surgery from the Medical College of Georgia in 1970. He interned at the City of Memphis Hospitals and the University of Tennessee, and he served his residency in general surgery at the University of Tennessee and his Fellowship in Orthopaedic Surgery at the Campbell Clinic in Memphis, Tennessee. He is a member of the American Academy of Orthopaedic Surgeons, the Georgia Medical Society, and the Bibb County Medical Society and specializes in shoulder surgery, hip and knee reconstruction, knee surgery, and back surgery.

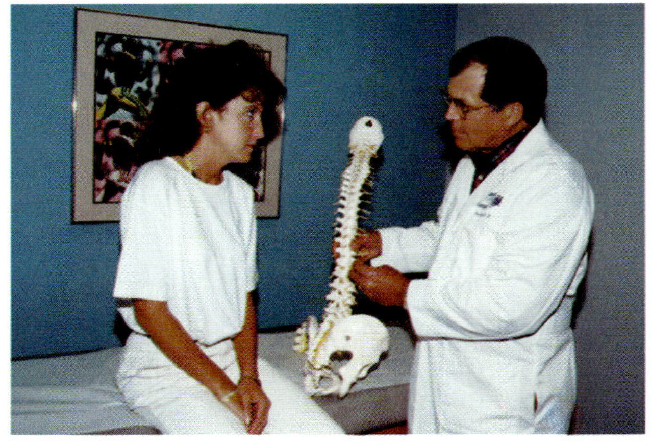

Dr. William S. Barnes graduated from Virginia Polytechnical Institute and the medical school at the Medical College of Georgia. He completed his internship and residency program at Greenville Hospital System in Greenville, South Carolina, and is a member of the American Academy of Orthopaedic Surgeons, the Bibb County Medical Society, the Georgia Medical Society, and the American Sports Medicine Fellowship Society. Dr. Barnes specializes in sports medicine, knee arthroscopy, shoulder surgery, hip and knee reconstruction, and back surgery.

Scott Hefner, president of A.T.A.R.I. (Athletic Therapy and Rehabilitation Institute), says his division of Piedmont is an outpatient orthopaedic facility that employs licensed athletic trainers, licensed physical therapists, and licensed massage therapists in his 10,000-square-foot, state-of-the-art facility that includes a 26-foot-long in-ground pool. "Rehabilitation is hard enough," he said, "so we try to accommodate with the ambiance of a relaxed atmosphere. We treat all ages—kids to senior citizens—and we treat any extremity—low back or neck injuries, and post-op cases of the same areas. All our patients are recommended by doctors—everyone who has rehabilitation here must have a doctor's referral." Hefner says A.T.A.R.I. conducts seminars for industry, school systems, and other organizations that have the need to know about signs of symptoms or injuries or conditions.

Dr. Jean M. Marine, specializing in hand and upper extremities, is one of Piedmont's most recent additions to staff. She graduated from the University of California, Berkeley, and from medical school at Tuft's University School of Medicine, in Boston. She served her internship and residency in general surgery and orthopedic surgery at the University of California, San Francisco. She also served residencies in orthopedic surgery at California Pacific Medical Center, San Francisco, and Hahnemann University Hospital in Philadelphia, and her fellowship in hand and upper extremity at the University of Alabama, Birmingham. She is certified by the American Board of Orthopedic Surgery and a member of the American Academy of Orthopedic Surgeons, Southern Orthopedic Association, Southern Medical Association, and American Medical Association.

Dr. Layne Myers, director of occupational medicine at Piedmont, says Piedmont's goal is to provide medical care to employers and employees. "The clinic in Warner Robins," he said, "was opened for the care of occupational medicine conditions and this practice has grown and prospered. At this time, care for the full spectrum of industrial and occupational medicine is offered. Working together with patients and with clients, the practice is adapting to changing corporate and individual patient needs." Myers says that Piedmont's progress has grown to include all facets of occupational medicine. "Our goal," he says, "is optimal and effective medical care. Responding to the employee's and the employer's needs in a timely fashion is a priority, and rehabilitation services also are available without delay at this same location."

At Piedmont, it is not only it goal to help get patients back to work at full capacity, but also to determine if they are suited for a particular job. These functional assessments are job and/or injury specific. At Piedmont, care providers want to get employees back on the job, just as doctors and trainers on the sidelines want to treat injured athletes and get them back in the game. Piedmont is the "sideline" physician or trainer that gets an employee back to work. It offers job site analysis, including ergonomics, pre-employment screening, injury prevention programs, functional capacity evaluations, and work conditioning programs. Piedmont believes that through prevention, care and management of injuries, and most important of all, communication between all parties involved, it can maximize every employee's functional abilities.

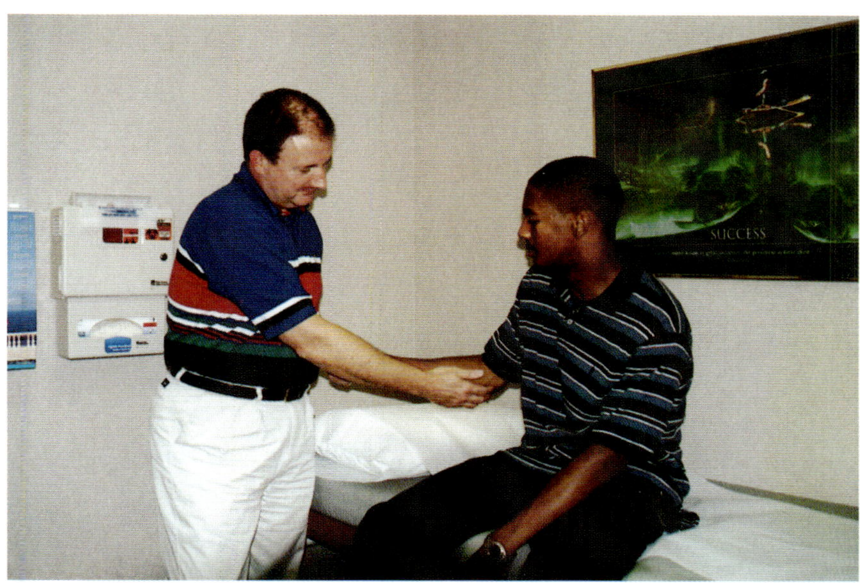

Whether one is 6 or 60-plus, when looking to Piedmont, everyone will find a team of physicians, registered nurses, certified athletic trainers, registered physical therapists, and rehabilitation therapists to help put "motion" back in every picture of life! ❋

SECURE HEALTH PLANS OF GEORGIA

At a time when insurance providers across the country are facing an industry in crisis, Secure Health Plans of Georgia offers the most efficient health-care delivery system. Secure Health provides comprehensive services to self-insured companies who want to contain rising health-care costs without sacrificing service to their employees.

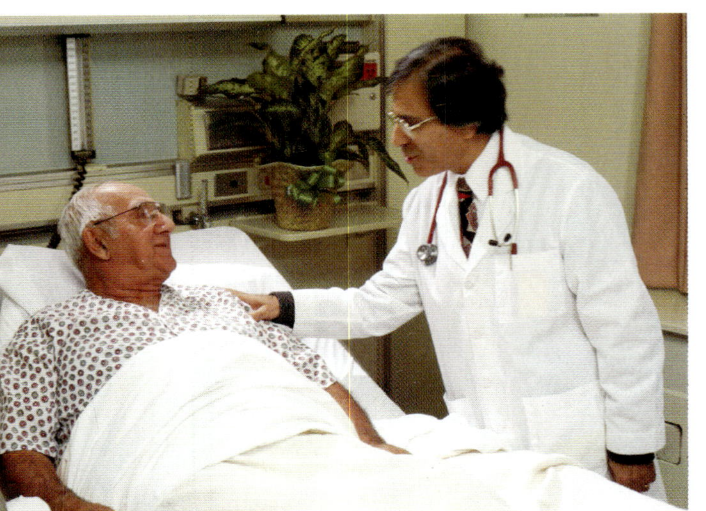

Over the last several years many health-care companies have tried unsuccessfully to manage costs by diminishing the service provided and by lowering their physicians' fee schedules. But, as a recent Towers Perrins industry report states, employers will continue to see average cost hikes ranging from 8 to 12 percent over the next few years.

George Israel, CEO of Secure Health, understands the report and agrees that the main concern in the industry is escalating costs. Israel points out some of the rising cost culprits: "Prescription drugs has to be one, outpatient utilization, perhaps abuse of emergency room, and some others we've got to get a handle on." Secure Health is dedicated to an integrated care strategy that eliminates duplication in order to lower costs, he added.

"We truly want to partner with employers for the long term, to build a lasting relationship of trust, respect, and reliability," explained Israel. "We want to help them identify cost issues within their plans and customize their plans in order to meet their particular benefits needs."

Secure Health's "one-stop shopping" scope of services is located all under one roof. Its main emphasis is the Preferred Provider Organization (PPO) network, which includes 700 physicians and 14 health-care facilities. This extensive network enables Secure Health to negotiate competitive rates with doctors and hospitals. These facilities include: Bleckley Memorial Hospital, Crisp Regional Hospital, Dodge County Hospital, HealthSouth Central Georgia Rehabilitation Hospital, Houston Medical Center, Jasper Memorial Hospital, The Medical Center of Central Georgia, Monroe County Hospital, Oconee Regional Medical Center, Peach Regional Medical Center, Perry Hospital, Putnam General Hospital, Taylor Regional Hospital, Taylor-Telfair Hospital, and Upson Regional Medical Center.

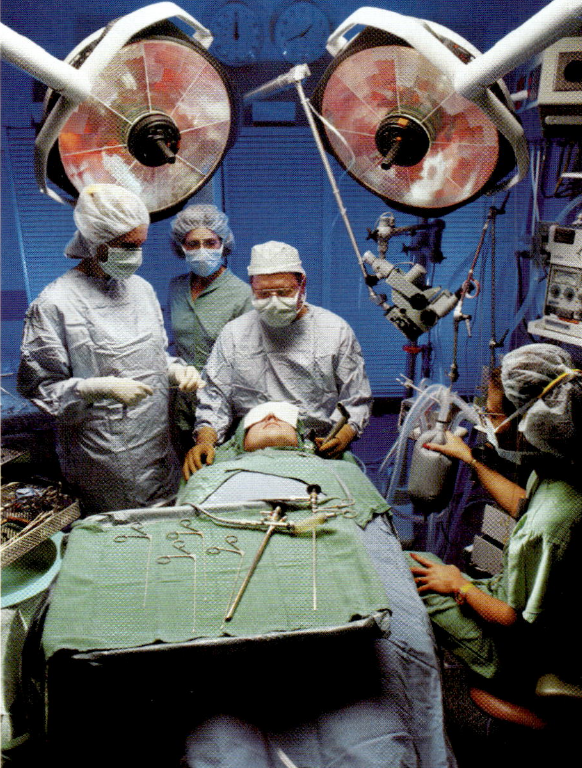

"Not only can our PPO enhance the benefit package for the employer, but we can administer their health-care plans as well," said Israel.

Secure Health offers full third-party administrative services (TPA). It pays medical, dental, and vision claims, plus performs COBRA administration on behalf of the employer's plan. Its professional staff of nurses works with doctors and facilities to pre-certify in-patient admissions and diagnostic procedures as required by many plans.

Secure Health also offers an Employee Assistance Program (EAP). The program allows employees to seek professional counseling services for themselves and family members for marital problems, addictions, and crisis intervention. It currently has more than 36,000 employees and dependents accessing EAP services.

Since the early '90s, Secure Health has provided PPO services to more than 55,000 employees and their dependents. Approximately 26,000 employees and dependents utilize the TPA services.

Secure Health's depth of services offers a statewide network option for employers with multiple locations. With the one-stop shopping capability, 99 percent accuracy rate in processing claims, local knowledge of area hospitals and physicians, and a highly experienced staff looking for ways to manage costs, Secure Health Plans of Georgia is a smoothly run operation.

Secure Health's professional commitment and dedication have earned the confidence of local companies as well as national corporations located in Georgia. Companies have customized their own health-care plans by working with Secure Health to develop innovative health-care initiatives.

As part of its partnership philosophy and commitment to the community, Secure Health has two employer representatives serving on its governing board. Local physicians and hospitals in Central Georgia own Secure Health.

Secure Health is located at 3920 Arkwright Road, Suite 405, in Highridge Center Office Complex in north Macon. For more information, call (912) 314-2400. ❋

• Photo by Ken Krakow

CHAPTER THIRTEEN

13

Manufacturing & Distribution

Photo by Ken Krakow

BROWN & WILLIAMSON TOBACCO CORPORATION

Unsurpassed . . . unique . . .world-class. Many companies lay claim to these titles; however, Brown & Williamson's manufacturing facility in Macon is truly an international leader when it comes to manufacturing. The plant is preeminent in the areas of safety, quality, and efficiency. Brown & Williamson meets global standards in a demanding economy while providing an environmentally friendly employer and civic-minded neighbor for Middle Georgians.

Its 1.4 million-square-foot facility—one of the largest cigarette manufacturing operations in the world—is situated on a 200-acre campus. The men and women there operate the most advanced machinery and technology within the industry, enabling them to respond to the rapid changes of an emerging global marketplace.

Brown & Williamson is the third largest cigarette manufacturer and marketer in the United States with a portfolio of brands to include Kool, Lucky Strike, Pall Mall, Capri, and Viceroy. Its roots began in 1894 when George Brown and Robert Williamson formed a partnership in Winston-Salem, North Carolina. Since 1927, the company has been a subsidiary of London-based British-American Tobacco, the world's foremost international cigarette manufacturer.

Brown & Williamson Tobacco Corporation's corporate headquarters are located in Louisville, Kentucky. The company also operates the industry's largest leaf tobacco processing facility in Wilson, North Carolina and a smaller manufacturing facility outside Richmond, Virginia, where sheet tobaccos are produced for use in cigarette manufacturing.

British-American Tobacco shares an ironic link with American Tobacco. British-American Tobacco was first established in 1902 as the international trading company of James Duke's American Tobacco Company in the United States and the Imperial Tobacco Company of Great Britain and Ireland. In 1911, the United States Supreme Court ruled the structure that created British-American Tobacco was illegal, and it became an independent company. Then, more than 90 years after being created, British-American Tobacco bought American Tobacco, in effect purchasing its former parent company.

In Macon, Brown & Williamson is one of Middle Georgia's largest private employers. Local operations include cigarette manufacturing, as well as several corporate functions. Cigarette manufacturing is managed by several departments, including Primary, Fabrication, and Shipping. Purchasing, Distribution, Engineering, and Research and Development are located in Macon to provide increased interaction between production and key related departments.

Brown & Williamson's Macon complex is tremendous. With 54 acres under roof, it contains its own power plant, wastewater treatment facility, and leaf storages warehouse.

The corporation's 90,000-square-foot Research and Development building adjacent to the main manufacturing facility is home to a diverse group of technical experts and scientists from over 20 countries.

The Research and Development department is responsible for the ongoing quality analysis and development of product improvements and innovations for Brown & Williamson.

The Engineering Department provides corporate-wide engineering services. With a staff of a diverse group of engineers and technicians, department responsibilities include facility design and construction, technology selection and application, process improvements, and management information services.

• (top) Brown & Williamson's facility is one of the largest and most modern cigarette manufacturing facilities in the world.

• (right) The atrium provides an excellent venue for company and employee events.

SAFETY IS THE TOP PRIORITY

Brown & Williamson's first responsibility is to provide a safe working environment for all its employees. The "Take 2/Buddy System" program was created by employees to insure the highest safety standards possible. Since the inception of this program there has been a dramatic reduction in the number of lost-time accidents, achieving the remarkable milestone of one million accident- and incident-free hours. This is the equivalent of 245 eight-hour workdays without a single lost-time accident and is a first in the facility's 23-year history. Because of the company's accomplishments in safety and its efforts to adhere to British-American Tobacco policies on environmental responsibility, it proudly accepted the first ever British-American Tobacco "Responsible Stewardship Award."

The near future holds even more accomplishments for Brown & Williamson's safety initiatives. The company recently received the "Merit" designation from OSHA's prestigious Voluntary Protection Program. This outstanding achievement puts Brown & Williamson on a short list of companies nationwide committed to safety.

QUALITY IS A WAY OF LIFE

Just as Brown & Williamson is determined to be a safe place to work, it is also driven to insure that quality is unnegotiable throughout the entire operation. From the primary area that utilizes one of the most advanced vision systems for foreign matter detection and removal, to the use of the Pack Vision System and the Integrated Operator interfaces in the fabrication area, Brown & Williamson is implementing sophisticated technologies to maintain product quality in every vital area of the manufacturing process. Its commitment to quality is further demonstrated by an ability to address the complexities of a growing international demand for its products.

The 88 different countries to which Brown & Williamson exports have specific and highly individual requirements for quality standards; in order to ensure the highest degree of quality and precision for these export markets, specialized teams have been organized to exclusively accommodate those needs. The culmination of its pursuit for unsurpassed quality will be obtained when its ISO registration process is completed for both the ISO 9000/2000 and ISO 14001 certification. When these two international standards are achieved, Brown & Williamson will be recognized as part of an elite group of highly efficient and quality conscious manufacturing facilities.

PERFORMANCE IS DRIVEN BY PEOPLE

Since the plant began operations in 1977, the manufacturing purpose of the facility has changed significantly. Originally, KOOL Filter Kings was the only product manufactured; today, the company routinely handles dozens of brands with hundreds of variations. Due to the competitive framework of the industry, Brown & Williamson has had to redefine and grow the facility so that it is able to immediately respond to rapidly changing domestic and international market demands.

As for the manufacturing of Brown & Williamson's world-class cigarettes, the company's quality leaf is stored until production scheduling calls for a certain amount of burley, flu-cured, or oriental tobacco. Entering the primary area, the tobacco undergoes a wonderful metamorphosis—changing from agricultural planting into a major component of a product enjoyed by millions of adult consumers around the world.

The tobacco is first conditioned, as it is brought to a specific moisture level in order to minimize waste. The conditioning also prepares the tobacco for the blending area where it is combined into specific mixtures to provide each brand's unique smoking characteristics. As the tobacco is taken from the blending area it is prepared for the casing area. Casing is a highly unique mixture of solids and liquids for each brand that provides some flavorings but also assures retail shelf life and freshness. Casing mixtures are specifically prepared for each separate brand and style of cigarette manufactured by Brown & Williamson.

The tobacco is then cut into narrow strands and dried so that the "working moisture" is removed. Additions—unique tobacco components—are then introduced into some blends before the tobacco is stored.

• (top) Advanced touch screen technology provides machine operators instant access to information.

• (left) High-speed and high-tech, but the emphasis is on quality... the consumer demands it!

Specialized quality controls are located throughout the entire primary process to ensure the right amount of moisture in the tobacco and to assure that the precise amount of casings and flavorings are applied. Vision systems attuned to learning colors are used in the cutting and drying area for removal of foreign matter. Primary has the capacity to produce enormous amounts of tobacco per day but the real emphasis is on quality, not quantity.

At the end of the primary process the custom-prepared blends are transferred to the fabrication floor where they are ready to be made into Brown & Williamson's world-class cigarettes.

In Fabrication, the newest generation of making, packing, and case packing machines can make and pack up to 14,000 cigarettes per minute without jeopardizing the quality of the product. Just as in Primary, there are many quality safeguards used throughout the fabrication process. The most advanced technology is used to improve quality and efficiency.

After leaving Fabrication, the finished product is sent to the shipping department and then on to the company's central distribution center.

Throughout the entire manufacturing plant floor, Brown & Williamson's assurance of the greatest productivity and quality is achieved in large part through a scientific approach to maintenance that utilizes programs such as vibration analysis and predictive maintenance procedures like ultrasound, thermography, and oil analysis. These programs, along with others, play a large part in making sure the entire manufacturing floor performs at optimum efficiency.

Brown & Williamson continually improves the manufacturing process to reduce waste and provide precision manufacturing at lightening-fast speed. Throughout the world there are no better quality products than those it produces.

In addition to Leaf Storages, Primary, Fabrication, and Shipping, Brown & Williamson Macon has added other key components essential to the manufacturing process. The Research and Development center moved to Macon in 1994. Research and Development employees address a wide range of consumer expectations about cigarette design, including filters, tobacco blends, and smoking characteristics. Members of Research and Development come from diverse academic backgrounds representing many areas of expertise.

Assisting Research and Development is the development center, a scaled-down version of the entire manufacturing process. Here, sample batches help Research and Development and Manufacturing to enhance process development and to conduct tests on new products. The staffs of both centers understand the complex nature of the industry and pride themselves on their ability to respond to the evolving demands of a worldwide market.

Brown & Williamson's Regional Data Center is responsible for handling all the company's Information Technology needs. More than 2,000 computer terminals are linked to an internal network via a fiber-optic backbone and administrated by a staff of highly experienced Information Technology professionals.

Brown & Williamson's plant is designed to manufacture the highest quality cigarettes in the world. But that would not be possible without many different departments throughout the facility supporting the manufacturing process. These departments include International Customer Service, Accounting and Finance, Human Resources and Employee Relations, Scheduling, Purchasing and Distribution, and Parts.

TAKING PRIDE IN THE COMMUNITY

Since coming to Macon in 1977, Brown & Williamson has formed a solid relationship with the community and the state of Georgia. Its economic impact in Georgia approaches $500 million per year. Just as important, though, are the civic contributions of the company and employees. As a result of its involvement, nearly $1 million is contributed annually to charitable agencies and organizations.

Brown & Williamson's companywide efforts to support the United Way and the United Negro College Fund receive nationwide attention, and through a wide variety of local programs, its employees

• (top) Where possible, the most advanced technology available enhances efficiency in the fabrication process.

• (right) An example of innovation, the shipping department utilizes robotics to sort and stack cases for shipment.

are able to make a significant impact in the community, while at the same time creating a positive image for Brown & Williamson.

Safety, Quality, Performance, and Community—Brown & Williamson is dedicated to all four of these principles both at its Macon facility and as a world leader in manufacturing. The men and women who comprise this excellent operation are committed to continually improving its products and services in order to become the preeminent leader in the manufacture of tobacco products.

TO LEARN MORE ABOUT BROWN & WILLIAMSON

In 1997, Brown & Williamson launched its Web site, www.brownandwilliamson.com. The Web site remains one of the most comprehensive resources for tobacco information on the Internet. Consumers worldwide can learn Brown & Williamson's position on the most current issues effecting the tobacco industry, including addiction, help for quitting smoking, research into alternative cigarette products, and environmental tobacco smoke. Please make use of this Web site to find additional information about Brown & Williamson. ❋

• (top) In Fabrication, prepared tobacco blends are combined with paper, filters, and packaging materials by a series of high-speed machines.

• (left) In Shipping, a computerized conveyor routing system organizes finished cases by product code.

YKK CORPORATION OF AMERICA

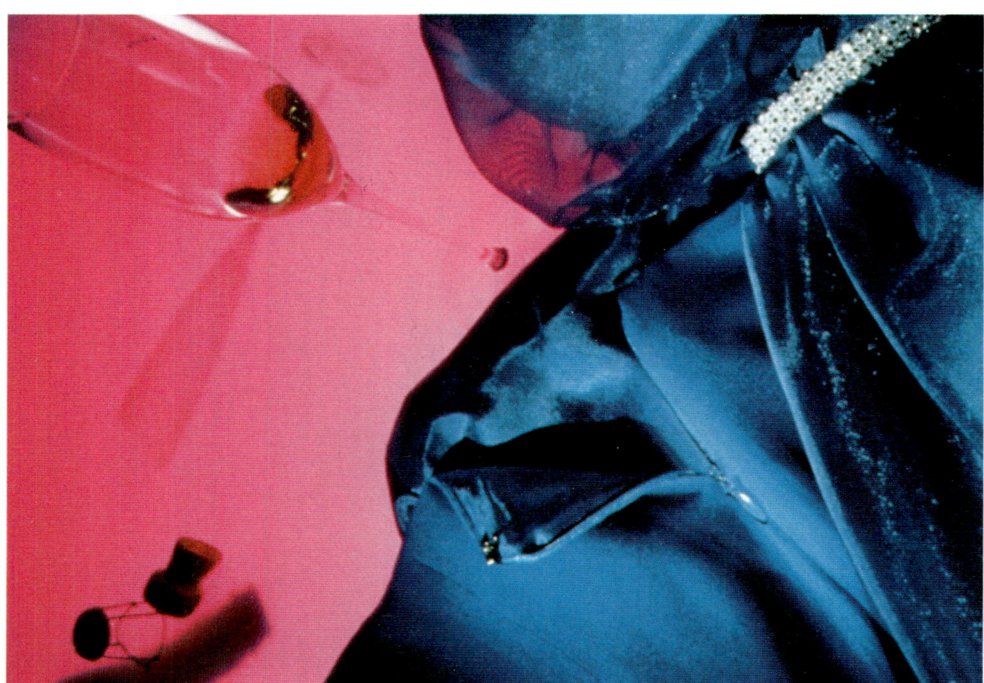

From its inception as a small company that began manufacturing zippers in 1934, YKK is now a major worldwide player in two industry categories: fasteners for sewn products and architectural aluminum building products.

Originally founded in Japan by Tadao Yoshida, YKK's mission is based on Mr. Yoshida's philosophy, which he called the "Cycle of Goodness." Simply stated, it means that no one prospers unless he renders benefit to others. Employees, customers, suppliers, and the local community are all participants in this Cycle.

In this spirit, YKK fuels the growth of its businesses and the quality of life for its many communities around the world via its own success. Beyond profits, an important aspect of YKK's goal is to spur economic growth, environmental well-being, and corporate involvement in any place that is home to a YKK facility.

Within YKK America Group, prosperity begins with research and development. Corporate philosophy dictates a heavy investment in R&D. From product and process improvement to market research and environmental impact, YKK employees are constantly engaged in the search for a better way. As a result of this single-minded devotion to continuous improvement, more than 8,000 items have been the object of patent applications and utility models under the YKK name. Whether in the categories of fasteners or architectural aluminum building products, the goals of the research and development arms of YKK have always been growth, discovery, and progress.

A penchant for product quality extends beyond the lab and into the production facilities and procedures in YKK plants worldwide. An example is YKK's unique Vertically Integrated Production System, a manufacturing method mandating that wherever feasible, YKK manufactures everything itself — utilizing the purest raw materials and the company's own facilities and expertise. For its 2.6-million-square-foot National Manufacturing Center in Macon, now the zipper-making complex in the entire world, YKK produces its own brass in order to ensure it's as close to perfect for zippers as possible.

At its Macon National Manufacturing Center, the company's innovations and breakthroughs are impressive. Modern artisans have turned the basic zipper into a product line that includes more than 1,500 metal and plastic styles in 427 standard colors. There are numerous one-of-a-kind value-added zippers — like the Illusion®, a zipper whose teardrop pull-tab has become the much sought-after symbol of excellence in designer dresses and skirts; or the very popular Vislon® brand, an injection-molded zipper with memory that is at once fashionable and durable.

Under the strong global leadership of the current president and founder's son, Tadahiro Yoshida, YKK began to diversify in the 1980s. North America was no exception. For example, YKK extended its fastener business beyond zippers. Today, its brand of self-fastening hook and loop tapes is SmartTouch®, a product that features an army of tiny nylon hooks designed to grab loops faster and hold tighter than any other woven hook and loop. The PowerHook® brand of injection molded hook comes in several heights depending on the application that's needed. And, the FastenMates™ brand is a line of colorful plastic buckles and notions seen in luggage as well as sporting goods.

Whatever the final application — from fish farm nets to gear for outer space — innovative YKK zippers are engineered to enhance product performance. YKK has become the industry leader, the one-source resource for a dizzying array of closure combinations and variations.

• (above) This dress features YKK's Illusion® zipper with its teardrop pull-tab — a much sought-after symbol of excellence.

• (right) At the YKK USA Brasswire Plant in Macon, Georgia, brass is produced to form basic zipper parts: zipper teeth, sliders, and top and bottom stops; plus fasteners for other YKK America Group Companies.

YKK even makes zippers for fastening together artificial turf football fields such as the one at the Georgia Dome.

An integral part of the YKK America Group family of companies is YKK Universal Fasteners Inc. (UFI). Acquired by YKK in 1987, UFI has manufacturing operations in Kentucky and Tennessee, where it produces metal buttons, snaps, Snapets®, rivets and burrs, and hooks and eyes. It also provides customers with the automated machinery necessary for attaching its fasteners.

In 1996, YKK purchased Tape Craft Corporation. Headquartered in Anniston, Alabama, Tape Craft increased its capacity in 1998 with a new state-of-the-art plant in Oxford, Alabama. Sharing many of its markets with YKK USA and UFI, Tape Craft manufactures nylon, polyester, polypropylene, and cotton webbings for a huge variety of applications.

More than 45 years ago, in an effort to competitively secure quality metals for zippers, YKK became involved in producing aluminum. What has resulted is an international architectural aluminum building-products business — YKK AP (for Architectural Products) — that now represents approximately two-thirds of the Company's total global sales.

YKK AP America Inc. operates a sprawling architectural aluminum plant in Dublin, Georgia. It's the only aluminum products manufacturing facility of its kind in the United States where every manufacturing step — from aluminum smelting to final fabrication — takes place under one huge roof.

The aluminum profiles of YKK AP can be found locally in the entrances, storefronts, window wall, or curtainwall systems of such prestige projects as the Cox Communications Building, as well as at the Georgia Music Hall of Fame, the Georgia Sports Hall of Fame, and the Peyton Anderson Foundation. They can also be seen in Atlanta at the Georgia Dome and Turner Field.

In this new century, YKK sees sweeping industry changes ahead and the resulting need for continued product and process improvement. Still, the things that matter most will stay firmly rooted and immutable: a firm commitment to quality and service, and the hard-earned trust of many satisfied customers. The "Cycle of Goodness," a never-ending spiral generating progressively better things for people and their world, will remain the cornerstone of YKK's mission. ❋

• (above left) YKK zippers, plus color-coordinated hook and loop add style and durability to this jacket.

• (left) Atlanta's Turner Field uses YKK AP aluminum to hold its glass windows and doors in place.

WALTHALL OIL COMPANY

Walthall Oil Company is a third-generation company that has been involved in the petroleum business for more than 50 years. Presently owned and operated by Frank Walthall III, president, Walthall Oil had its beginning in 1952 when Walthall's father, Frank Walthall Jr. bought half interest in Thames Oil Company from Joel Thames. At that time, the company became Thames & Walthall Oil Company. "My father, who died in 1997, bought out Thames' interest in the early 1960s, and the company's name changed to Walthall Oil Company," said Frank Walthall III. "Actually, my grandfather, Frank Walthall Sr., was involved in the oil business too, working with Pure Oil, as my father did before he bought into Thames Oil Company."

Walthall, who is proud of his company's family business legacy, began working at Walthall Oil when he was 12, joining up full time after he graduated from Georgia Tech in 1979. One of his own sons, Malcolm, is a high school student who has also taken an interest in the business and works there part-time. His 12-year-old son, Wesley, is also looking forward to working in the business.

Originally located on Vineville Avenue, in 1988 Walthall Oil Company moved to its present state-of-the-art facility, which houses its corporate offices at 2510 Allen Road. In addition to this plant, the company has another Macon location, as well as one in Thomaston. The three warehouses have a combined total of 22,000 square feet. "That means," said Walthall, "the products our customers want are on hand and in excellent condition, waiting to be delivered when our customers need them."

"Our company," said Walthall, "is the largest locally based distributor of its kind in the Middle Georgia area. We supply all your petroleum needs—from products to equipment to services. We also provide industrial plant lubrication surveys, and we go all the way to Augusta, Columbus, Valdosta, and Atlanta, and all points in between."

Walthall Oil Company offers a complete line of 300 products including gasoline, diesel, kerosene, solvents, lubricants, synthetics, industrial oils and greases, and environmental products. The company provides all types of lubricants, including synthetic lubricants from ExxonMobil, Chevron, and other companies. Catering to customers whose needs are as varied as the company's inventory, Walthall Oil sells to walk-ins, as well as to major companies. Walthall said his company's products are available in a variety of quantities. "We can sell you a quart of oil or we can refill your million gallon standby fuel tank. We can also handle your special requests. Due to the fact that we do business with several major oil companies, we can get what you need, when you need it. And, if you need equipment, we can provide that also."

Walthall Oil Company is a regional supplier and is able to help its customers wherever they are located, even if they are outside the Middle Georgia area. The company's bulk plant in Macon is located directly across the street from two major pipeline terminals, and it also pulls products from terminals in several cities across the state—from Atlanta, Savannah, Augusta, Griffin, Americus, and Albany. With an overall employment of over 200 people, Walthall Oil Company operates a modern fleet of delivery trucks that are on

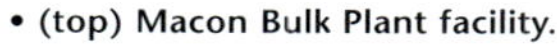
• (top) Macon Bulk Plant facility.

• (bottom) Two of Walthall Oil's modern fleet.

the road all day, every day. To ensure the delivery of quality products, the company has dedicated tank wagons for bulk lubricants, kerosene, and mineral spirits. It has its own maintenance team and trucks that are on call 24 hours a day. "Our drivers are first class," said Walthall. "Each one has an excellent safety record and years of driving experience."

At Walthall Oil, customers come first, "because," as Walthall said, "we wouldn't be here if it weren't for them. We also believe in our staff. We take care of our employees so they can take care of our customers. Our sales team is helpful, friendly, and experienced. Our management staff is progressive. We are not a one-person organization; we are a team, and you can count on us to understand your business and help you plan for the future."

Walthall Oil Company presently operates 15 convenience stores located throughout middle and South Georgia. Being the first company to introduce fast pay credit at the pump island, Walthall now has this service available at all its company-operated stores. In addition, at Walthall's unattended proprietary FLEET 24 wholesale sites, customers can pump their own fuel 24 hours a day, 7 days a week, and receive valuable management tracking reports on their usage and mileage. Walthall also uses electronic funds transfer, satellite communications, electronic data interchange, computer-aided tank monitoring and inventory control, and the Internet to make it easy for customers to do business with them.

Walthall Oil Company provides a full range of management consulting services. These services include assisting with fuel tax compliance, handling customers' environmental upgrades, helping manage its customers' retail gasoline or convenience store business, and planning image and facility enhancements.

"We believe in helping our community," Frank Walthall said. "We have the knowledge and the expertise to respond in all types of emergencies, no matter how great or small. Whether it's making a delivery in the snow or assisting a disaster, our customers can always count on us when the going gets tough."

During the flood of '94, Walthall Oil gave out three truck loads of free water at its retail stores and also provided drums filled with water to the Methodist Children's Home on Pierce Avenue. This community-minded company also helped an elderly lady make needed home repairs for Christmas in April in 1999 and has been involved with the Department of Family & Children's Services to provide Christmas gifts to underprivileged children.

Walthall Oil Company, which has been in the petroleum business for over 50 years, can supply all petroleum needs—from products to equipment to services. To find out more about this third-generation company and the services and products it provides, visit its Web site at www.walthall-oil.com. ✷

• (top) 4433 Forsyth Road Exxon.

• (left) Ocmulgee East Boulevard at I-16 truck stop/restaurant.

PACTIV

The Macon facility is part of Pactiv Corporation (formerly Tenneco Packaging), a $3-billion company based in the Chicago area. Pactiv Corporation was spun off from Tenneco, Inc. in November 1999 to become a stand-alone packaging company. Pactiv manufactures food and industrial packaging and consumer products, including Hefty® waste bags and Hefty® OneZip storage bags. The Macon facility is part of Pactiv's molded fibre business, which manufactures egg packaging, cup carriers, paper plates, and industrial packaging from recycled paper.

Groundbreaking for the Macon facility took place in August 1966. Since then, the plant has provided steady employment for the area. Presently 240 employees work in production, maintenance, sales, and administrative positions in Macon. Numerous local suppliers have nourished mutually beneficial relationships with the plant.

Macon is the largest of Pactiv's egg packaging manufacturing sites. The site manufactures 12- and 18-egg cartons and egg trays on five production lines. The plant's four-shift operation maintains a 7-day/week, 24-hour/day schedule, turning out an average of 1.5 million cartons and trays per day. Every year it recycles nearly 40,000 tons of newspaper and other post-consumer paper into useful egg packaging.

The Macon facility is recognized as the premier egg packaging manufacturer in the world. The excellent motivated local workforce gives it an advantage over the competition. ISO quality certification has locked in best practices and provides for continuous improvement. The plant has numerous citations for its excellent safety and operational performance.

The plant's local 130,000-square-foot warehouse provides storage for inventory in the summer months to meet high demand for egg packaging at Christmas and Easter.

From Macon, the plant ships to egg packers throughout the U.S.A. Environmentally friendly, Pactiv packaging can be found nearly everywhere eggs are sold. Pactiv counts Kroger and Wal-Mart among its biggest customers.

Pactiv Macon is one of the oldest continuing businesses in the Macon area and looks forward to a bright future in egg packaging! ❋

BURGESS PIGMENT CO.

The Burgess family knows kaolin.

In 1880, John W. Burgess owned a clay mine in Hockessin, Delaware. In 1917, John Burgess III co-owned a kaolin company in Dry Branch, Georgia. As a youth, Malcolm Burgess Sr.'s first job was carrying 10-gallon buckets of water to kaolin miners in Dry Branch. He continued to work there on and off over the next few years while finishing high school and attending Brewton Parker College, and in 1930 at 23 years of age, he was put in charge as plant superintendent.

In 1945, Malcolm's wife Nell encouraged him to start his own company. Taking that advice, he founded Burgess-Washington Clays. Three years later in September of 1948, he founded Burgess Pigment Company and over four decades later Burgess Pigment Company is one of the leaders of its field in producing calcined clay.

Malcolm Burgess Jr. followed in his family's footsteps, and in 1961, he began spending his summer breaks from school at his father's business. In 1971, after receiving a BSBA degree from the University of North Carolina and serving in the U.S. Army for three years, he returned to Georgia and began working at Burgess Pigment Company full-time. Since his father's retirement in March of 1991, Malcom Jr. has taken over as president and chief executive officer of the corporation and has continued to lead the company from its humble beginnings in 1948 to where it is today—a multimillion-dollar business. His son, Sandy Burgess, who received a degree in business administration from Furman University and a MBA degree from the University of Georgia, joined the company in 1999.

Kaolin is a naturally occurring mineral formed during the glacial period of America and its rich deposits in Georgia helped to make the state the leading producer of the clay.

Burgess Pigment Company processes hydrous kaolin by removing the water from the mineral using high-temperature furnaces, which run continuously 24 hours a day, 7 days a week. With 161 full-time employees working four shifts, the kaolin is treated using a highly technical process that requires constant monitoring. With the help of computer technology, it is classified by particle size, brightness, and functionality. A typical fine particle of kaolin is less than two microns thick or 40 times smaller than the eye can see. The kaolin, in dry form, is then ready to be delivered to the customer. Thousands of tons of kaolin are processed through Burgess Pigment each year.

With the production end of the business located in the heart of Washington County and the executive officers located on Pierce Avenue in Macon, Burgess Pigment Company doesn't stop there. It proudly ships its product to major corporations around the world. Its product can be found in a variety of forms used in the manufacturing of paint, wire and cable, rubber, plastics, adhesives, ceiling tile, floor moldings, cement, and make-up.

Burgess Pigment has gone from processing a few hundred tons of kaolin in 1948 to producing many thousand tons of clay today without ever leaving behind the family values that it was founded on. From Malcolm Sr.'s original vision for the future and Malcolm Jr.'s and Sandy's leadership abilities and expertise in kaolin, Burgess Pigment Company will continue to provide its customers with a high-quality product for generations to come. ❋

BOEING COMPANY

Many companies tout their presence in the communities in which they operate. They foster long associations with the town's people and herald their ties, support, and contributions to the community. But, no other company can lay claim to some of the very special relationships that exist, and certainly not the longevity of that relationship that exists between the people of Boeing, the United States, and Macon, Georgia.

From birch and canvas bi-planes, passenger liners, fighter jets, and military airlifters to the space shuttle, the people of Boeing, Boeing North American, and McDonnell Douglas share a common heritage. Combined, they have created much of the world's aviation history.

In early 1981, the U.S. Air Force announced that the McDonnell Douglas Corporation won the contract to build the C-17 airlifter, the most versatile large transport in the world. The C-17 is the first military transport to enter the U.S. Air Force service in more than two decades. The C-17 significantly modernized the U.S. airlift force and provided new capabilities for direct delivery of cargo and troops to auspicious airfields. The C-17 is the right aircraft at the right time with all the capabilities needed in our changing world.

To support this effort, the McDonnell Douglas Corporation expanded its operations to Macon in June of 1988. Initially, the work at the 200,000-square-foot Macon plant was 60 percent commercial (MD 80) and 40 percent military (C-17). In 1992, a decision was made to transfer out commercial and build only a military product.

Subsequently, a second building was opened in late 1994 to accommodate administration, procurement, inventory stores, and production. In August of 1997, the two aerospace giants, McDonnell Douglas and Boeing, merged to form the world's largest aircraft company. Today, the Macon plant builds 29 percent of the C-17 airlifters.

The 750 Boeing teammates in Macon work in the forefront of aircraft technology to support the United States' defense goals. Additionally, they work to support the community in which they live, giving countless hours and monetary support to many local civic, cultural, educational, and charitable organizations.

A cornerstone of the Boeing philosophy is taking an active part in community activities through employee participation in community service and corporate philanthropy. In addition to individual and corporate support, both the employee community funds and the Boeing Company are major contributors to the community. Recipients of their efforts include students of the Cynthia Weir Elementary School, where Boeing teammates are involved in tutoring students and encouraging them to remain in school. Boeing is involved in the Georgia Youth Science and Technology Center at the Museum of Aviation, Middle Georgia Youth Apprenticeship Program, Georgia Children's Home, American Red Cross, American Heart Association, the Museum of Aviation, Macon Chamber of Commerce, United Way, March of Dimes, membership on local advisory boards for area colleges, technical schools, and many more.

The key to the outstanding performance of the Macon facility is the highly motivated, well-trained, self-directed workforce operating in an environment of continuous improvement.

The highly trained workforce is the result of a public/private industry partnership with the Georgia Department of Technical and Adult Education. A standardized aerospace curriculum has been adopted at technical schools statewide to enhance training.

The objective of the Boeing Macon facility is to grow its business into a well-trusted and respected supplier of structural assemblies known throughout the corporation as the best value provider of these products.

For over 90 years, the Boeing Company has been a leader in the aerospace industry, an integral part of the community, and a good corporate citizen. Team Macon is proud to be part of this outstanding heritage. ✹

CHARLIE WOOD IMAGEWEAR

Charlie Wood Imagewear, in downtown Macon at 484 Second Street, evolved from Charlie Wood Sporting Goods, an old Middle Georgia business. The late Charlie Wood Sr., who established the company in 1950, supplied all the local school programs as well as clients all over the state with athletic equipment. "He helped many schools and organizations start and build their athletic programs," said his son, John Wood. "Since he had been in this type of business since 1932, he helped guide quite a few people through their careers."

John Wood, armed with three degrees in psychology and beginning his own career, decided to move back home to help his father with the changing business of embellished sportswear. Wood, who opened the Imagewear division in 1987, said, "we started assisting corporations and other businesses to enhance their image and employee relations by supplying them with shirts, caps, jackets, and other items that they would give their customers and employees. Although Imagewear had previously supplied sportswear for school fundraising, festivals (such as Macon's own Cherry Blossom Festival), races, and other types of events, John decided to add other categories and concentrate completely on decorated sportswear—and drop athletics.

Wood said that his company offers both screenprinted and embroidered sportswear, including caps, tote bags, and outerwear. "We're the only one that can do the real intricate work that many prefer," he said. "Our customers also include family reunions and college events, but, increasingly, complete garment programs for companies. We supply the reason, the organization, and the supply, so that very little of their time is necessary. Once we start a client, they usually stay with us because of our top-quality product, fair pricing, and guaranteed delivery. Some of our competitors regard us as the best in the state."

All of Imagewear's design and production is done at the business —making this an all-inclusive experience. "We've been called artists and designers who just happen to use shirts as our canvas," Wood said. "Because we generally approach our customers with ideas and products designed especially for them, they regard Imagewear as part of their marketing team. This is all very flattering and probably explains why we have such a loyal clientele."

Wood attributes much of his company's success to his employees who, he said, "have decided to make this their career choice. They are well-trained, loyal, good people, and one of them has been here 50 years." Wood said that his company has the most up-to-date equipment, such as an automatic press that can print 800 shirts an hour, in the area.

Unlimited embroidery decoration is also a strong feature at Charlie Wood Imagewear. "We have in-house sales representatives as well as reps around the state," Wood said. "We have an excellent reputation, and we want everything we do to enhance that reputation. Unique and attractive designs on shirts and other sportswear are the best advertisement we have. Our toll-free number is printed on all our shirts and this promotes quite a few calls after every major job."

Wood said his new computer system will allow his company "to tie all of our departments together and allow more designated marketing efforts. This will allow customers to be contacted more often and be kept up-to-date about special offers."

Charlie Wood Imagewear is very excited about its new Web site, which will make specific use of targeted e-mails. "We're trying to make shirt buying as easy as ordering anything else by using database-driven interactive ordering," Wood said. "This site should be unlike anything seen before in our business."

Next year, Charlie Wood Imagewear may just double its 2000 sales. For more information, call Charlie Wood Imagewear at 1-800-992-2104, or visit its Web site at www.imagewearcw.com. ❋

• John Wood, son of founder Charlie Wood Sr., proudly displays his company's products.

CHAPTER FOURTEEN

14

Marketplace, Tourism, & Quality of Life

Photo by Ken Krakow

MACON CENTREPLEX

When the clock struck midnight on December 31, 1999, it not only signaled the end of another year, another century, and another millennium, it also kicked off a promise of continued success for Macon's award-winning, state-of-the-art multi-purpose convention and entertainment facility known simply as the Macon Centreplex.

Although parts of the Macon Centreplex—the Macon Coliseum and the Macon City Auditorium—had been around for many decades, it wasn't until the facility's new Edgar H. Wilson Convention Centre burst onto the meetings and convention scene in 1996, that the ball really started rolling. Years of feasibility studies and research had shown a need for expanded convention and meeting facilities in the Middle Georgia area and anyway one looked at it, it certainly appeared such an expansion would be a wise move.

And a wise move it was. Since completing the major $20-million construction and renovation project that improved upon both the Coliseum and Auditorium and added the 102,000-gross-square-foot Convention Centre, facility management has seen the center meet and surpass expectations.

"Since opening the convention center in the spring of 1996, we have more than doubled our event numbers," said Centreplex General Manager Regina McDuffie. "And our event schedule just seems to keep growing."

According to McDuffie, the complex actually hosted some 1,060 different events for 1,289 event days during the facility's first full year of operation. Total attendance for the same period surpassed the quarter-million mark with 781,333 people passing through the facility's doors. Prior to the expansion, the facility averaged just 350 to 400 events annually.

As for the types of events held at the Centreplex, they are extremely varied. From local civic clubs, corporate meetings, and private parties, to major, multi-day conventions and various entertainment shows, the center entered the new millennium sustaining its claim to being one of the most flexible in the southeastern United States. Hosting a hockey game or concert, a major tradeshow, a number of small seminars and meetings, as well as a 1,000-plus banquet simultaneously has become commonplace. And, the facility's prime location in Macon, the very heart of the state where I-75 and I-16 meet, certainly hasn't hurt matters either as state and regional associations and organizations quickly began to realize great convenience and increased participation.

With the addition of the Convention Centre, the Macon Centreplex became the largest convention/event venue outside of metro-Atlanta. The center itself is attached to the Macon Coliseum and increased the Centreplex's available exhibit and meeting space almost three-fold to more than 120,000 gross square feet. It has a 30,800-square-foot exhibit hall, a 9,000-square-foot ballroom, a 3,400-square-foot full-service catering kitchen, and 18 other meeting and breakout rooms ranging in size from just over 350 square feet to more than 7,000 square feet.

Contributing further to the facility's flexibility, the exhibit hall and ballroom were designed for increased breakout ability and can be subdivided into two and five separate spaces, respectively. Additionally, the exhibit hall can be opened up into both the ballroom and the Coliseum Arena for more then 85,000 square feet of contiguous floor space.

The Coliseum Arena, which opened in 1968, and the City Auditorium, circa 1925, also underwent major renovations during the latter half of the 1990s, and both facilities entered the new millennium with renewed spirit.

The first venue of its size and type in the state, the Macon Coliseum has hosted full-house crowds for show

• (above) The Macon City Auditorium, a facility of the Macon Centreplex, stands tall. This grandiose building was built in 1925 and completely refurbished in 1998.

• (right) The Centreplex Coliseum is Macon and Middle Georgia's entertainment center! Built in 1968, it was the first facility of its size and type in the state and has hosted full-house crowds for show-business greats like Elvis, The Jacksons, Billy Joel, Reba McEntire, and Elton John! In addition to concerts and family shows, the Coliseum is the perfect site for a variety of events from conventions and trade shows to basketball, ice shows, circuses, and just about any other sporting or entertainment event imaginable.
Photos by Ken Krakow

business greats such as Elvis Presley, Michael Jackson, and Reba McEntire and finished up the 20th Century just as popular as ever. With more than 9,000 seats, the coliseum continues to host a variety of entertainment events as well as conventions, consumer trade shows, and sporting events such as hockey and basketball.

The coliseum's prime tenant since 1996 has been the Macon Whoopee, a professional team affiliated with the Central Hockey League. The team, which actually existed in Macon for one year back in the late '60s, returned to Macon in grand style, playing as many as 35 home games per year in front of record crowds.

The third facility of the Macon Centreplex—the Macon City Auditorium—is located in the heart of the historic district of downtown Macon. It is listed on the National Register of Historic Places and creates a very intimate and elegant atmosphere for a variety of events from large convention assemblies and public shows and concerts to banquets, private parties, and wedding receptions.

About the size of the Parthenon in Rome, Italy, and circular in plan, the auditorium is a study in state architecture with a Doric-style limestone colonnade surrounding three sides at the balcony level and a unique copper dome which is reportedly the largest in the world. The facility's "Great Hall" seats a total of 2,688 people and is accented above the stage with a breathtaking mural depicting Macon's history, from DeSoto's visit in 1540 to World War One.

So what about the new millennium? What does the Macon Centreplex's future hold?

Well, although the management is very proud of what has been accomplished in past decades, they aren't ready to sit back and relax.

"I would like to see the continued expansion of our market to bring more people into the Middle Georgia area," said McDuffie. "Convention and tourism—major economic assets for any city fortunate enough to attract them—are definitely on the upswing and represent the wave of the future.

"I also envision the development of the site directly across from our facility on Coliseum Drive to include a business-class hotel with additional meeting rooms and an open shopping area as well as a walking trail that connects the Ocmulgee Monument," McDuffie continued. "The original building was built as a replica of the Ocmulgee Indian mounds and I think it would be wonderful to redefine that connection." ❋

• (above) This aerial photograph shows the Macon Centreplex Coliseum and Convention Centre, located at 200 Coliseum Drive in Macon, Georgia. When used together, these two facilities offer convention and trade show planners more than 85,000 square feet of contiguous floor space.

• (left) The Macon Centreplex's Convention Centre, officially known as the Edgar H. Wilson Convention Centre, includes a 30,800-square-foot subdividable Exhibition Hall, a 9,100-square-foot subdividable Ballroom, and 14 additional meeting rooms. Photos by Ken Krakow.

CROWNE PLAZA MACON

The beautiful, upscale Crowne Plaza Hotel sits in the heart of historic downtown Macon at 108 First Street and is just minutes from all that Macon has to offer. Built in the early 1970s as a Hilton Hotel, it has been a part of the Crowne Plaza hotel chain since 1995. The Crowne Plaza Macon represents the merging of the past and the present.

The 297-room Crowne Plaza Macon underwent renovation of its rooms in 1997 and remodeling of its public areas the following year. It is beautifully decorated and landscaped and features a three-tiered water fountain with cobblestone circular drive at the entrance. Beautiful plants are strategically placed in the atrium and throughout the hotel. The hotel also offers a swimming pool overlooking the city, a four-level parking garage, state-of-the-art security cameras, room service, and a gift shop.

The two executive floors—the 15th and 16th floors—have special elevator key access and upgraded amenities and services including an extended Continental breakfast and evening cocktails in the concierge lounge. The four executive suites on the 16th floor each feature a large living room and dining room adjacent to a four-poster king bedroom. Balconies in each room overlook many of Macon's historical churches and mansions. The five junior suites on the second and third floors offer a guestroom and an adjacent separate parlor.

• The beautiful, upscale Crowne Plaza Hotel sits in the heart of historic downtown Macon at 108 First Street and is just minutes from all that Macon has to offer.

The Crowne Plaza Macon offers over 20,000 square feet of meeting space and can accommodate groups as small as 10 or as large as 1,500. The Preservation Hall Ballroom, with its multiple chandeliers, offers big-city elegance. The hotel also pays tribute to Macon's history with its Lanier Room, named for famed Macon poet Sidney Lanier, and the Mercer and Wesleyan rooms, honoring the city's two historic colleges.

For dining and socializing, the hotel offers a number of options. The Riverside Café, featuring American fare, is open for breakfast and lunch, and the hotel's new fine dining restaurant, open for dinner only, features an enticing menu. There's also the Big Easy Lounge featuring sandwiches and appetizers.

"The Crowne Plaza Macon is the only upscale hotel in Macon and Middle Georgia," said Dana Childress, Director of Sales and Marketing. "Its central Georgia and downtown Macon location results in a big economic impact on the city; yet our prices are less expensive than in many other areas. Government and association groups can afford to have their meetings and conventions here at this prime location in the center of the state." She said the hotel is focusing on hosting more and more local corporate business and government and association groups in the future.

Not only conveniently located in the center of the state, the Crowne Plaza Macon's proximity to the many downtown historic sites and the Georgia Music Hall of Fame, the Georgia Sports Hall of Fame, and the Harriet Tubman Museum makes it a likely destination for travelers to Macon.

The 16-story Crowne Plaza Macon is proud of its professional and friendly staff. Business and leisure travelers, conference attendees, and social guests can expect courtesy and efficiency, with a touch of Southern charm. ❋

COLONIAL MALL MACON

In a wooded area near an old fishing pond in 1975, a builder with a dream brought Middle Georgia their first and only super-regional shopping mall. The developer with such great vision was Colonial Properties, Inc., and 25 years later, Colonial Mall Macon is still owned and operated by Colonial Properties Trust and now lays claim to the title of the largest mall in the state with six department stores. One of the South's premier malls, Colonial Mall Macon has developed a deep community connection that spans a quarter of a century long, and a 32-county trade area wide.

When it opened in 1975, Macon Mall quickly became the area's retail and community hub. Several renovations and remodels, one major expansion, and a name-change later, Colonial Mall Macon still proudly offers the area's most complete selection of national and local retailers in a family-friendly environment.

Colonial Mall Macon houses over 200 retailers and brings the nation's top names to Macon with stores like Gap, Old Navy, Ann Taylor Loft, Eddie Bauer, The Disney Store, Limited, and Abercrombie & Fitch. Local merchants and seasonal operators bring a unique flavor to the mall. Serious shoppers appreciate such a huge selection of stores, and even the most hesitant customer feels at home in the mall's friendly atmosphere. Whether it's a collector browsing at an antique show, a teenager checking out the latest styles at a high-energy fashion show, or a parent watching his child ride the Venetian carousel, a shopper's time is always well-spent at Colonial Mall Macon.

Colonial Mall Macon also plays a vital role in Macon's economy. Yearly store sales contribute over $5.3 million in local and local-option sales taxes, while real-estate taxes total nearly $1.3 million annually. Payroll for the mall's 4,000 plus employees will also filter over $90 million into the Middle Georgia economy each year. Any observer can see the magnetic effect the mall has had on development along Eisenhower Parkway and Mercer University Drive.

Always a good corporate citizen, Colonial Mall Macon supports many non-profit groups through donations, special events, and fundraisers. Organizations such as the Muscular Dystrophy Association, Salvation Army, Make-A-Wish Foundation, Georgia Children's Museum, Children's Miracle Network, Macon Symphony Orchestra, and St. Jude's Children's Hospital are some of the many who have benefited from strong relationships with Colonial Mall Macon.

Colonial Mall Macon was named such because of an outstanding commitment made by Colonial Properties Trust to manage and maintain the mall with the highest standards in the industry.

Colonial Mall Macon will continue to offer customers a unique shopping experience and will exceed all of the community's expectations throughout the 21st century. Colonial Properties Trust is the largest diversified Real Estate Investment Trust in the nation. Its portfolio contains retail, multifamily, and office properties throughout the Southeast, including Colonial Grand at Wesleyan, Colonial Grand at Spring Creek, Colonial Grand at Barrington, Club and Colonial Village at North Ingle, all in Macon.

Colonial Mall Macon is proud of its commitment and contributions to the Macon community, and as it celebrates its 25th anniversary in the year 2000, it says "Thank You" to all who have joined in along the way. ❋

• (top) Colonial Mall Macon is the second largest mall in the state, housing over 200 retailers including six department stores.

• (left) One of the South's premier malls, Colonial Mall Macon has developed a deep community connection that spans a quarter of a century long, and a 32-county trade area wide.

NEWTOWN MACON

THE VISION

In 1823, James Webb visualized a beautiful city in a park. Where generously wide boulevards with lush linear parks accented charming storefronts. Where welcoming benches beckoned passersby to pause beneath the restful shade of a nearby tree and watch birds splash in a briskly flowing fountain. Webb's master plan for Macon, referred to as "New Town," included these aesthetically appealing features along with a design for living and growing that has weathered the test of time.

And with time comes changes and challenges. Almost 175 years later, Webb's grand and glorious vision is still visible, but through social and physical pressures the original luster of downtown Macon is tarnished. Architecturally significant buildings stand in need of renewal. Public services are in need of enhancement. Challenging transportation issues are in need of resolution.

NewTown Macon, Inc., plans to restore our city in a park to its original beauty and vitality. Envision downtown Macon's future with us.

Live in a city with a vigorous, prosperous, and diverse business climate.

Visit a city where parking is convenient, and getting from place to place is enjoyable.

Walk down tree-lined Cherry Street and admire beautifully restored buildings filled with offices, cafes, shops, and loft apartments.

Ride your bike on trails along the Ocmulgee River. See historic landmarks and pristine fish and wildlife preserves.

Work, shop, or live in a mixed-use riverside development.

Relax in a park nestled on the bank of the Ocmulgee River as children frolic in a nearby playground.

This is the collective vision of our community. Macon, Georgia, will soon be recognized as one of America's great cities. The renaissance of downtown is not merely a wish or hope. It is a viable, practical possibility when we as future-minded citizens capture the vision.

"Every resident, regardless of social status or economic background, will be able to feel they have a stake in downtown. This is an important time for Macon. We should feel proud of what we are doing in downtown. Every citizen will benefit."

- Virgil Adams, Newtown Macon board member.

• (top) Proposed riverside development.

• (below) A new restaurant in Anne's Tick Tock where Little Richard began singing.

THE PARTNERSHIP

In 1996, a group of visionary business and community leaders established a non-profit public-private partnership called NewTown Macon to fill a pressing community need: the development and facilitation of an integrated approach for revitalizing downtown Macon.

NewTown Macon's sole purpose is to facilitate change by marshaling leadership and providing support for projects that are important to our community. For four years, NewTown Macon has studied and identified the downtown area's most pressing economic and social needs. Subsequently, we collaborated with urban planners, development consultants, local organizations, governments, and citizens to develop a blueprint for the renaissance of downtown Macon that will spur significant economic growth and improve our quality of life.

NewTown Macon's revitalization plans include: the Urban Design Center; the Ocmulgee Heritage Greenway, a seven mile river walk; a $25 million mixed-use riverfront development; the restoration of Terminal Station as a passenger rail hub enhanced city entrances, streetscapes, public places, parking, and transportation; a programmed and signature Cherry Street Plaza; a downtown landscape and public amenity maintenance endowment; and a transitional property acquisition fund.

THE CHALLENGE

A New Century is upon us. Middle Georgian's are excited about the future of our city and our way of life. In his book *Cities Reborn, A Vision for Urban America*, William Hudnut, former mayor of Indianapolis, noted that a vibrant central city is critical to offering citizens a solid quality of life and competitive edge in the world economy. *"It is my belief that the future of the 21st-century city depends on the ability or failure of public, private, and not-for-profit leadership to meet these challenges."*

In 1999, a community challenge was issued. The Robert W. Woodruff and Peyton Anderson Foundations issued a challenge that calls upon all of this community's government constituencies, individuals, corporations, and foundations to come together for the greater good of our city and its future. Each foundation has issued a $3 million challenge grant toward the renaissance of downtown Macon. To claim this $6 million, our community is raising an additional $30 million.

A New Town will evolve. Many of the ingredients for a prosperous future are in place. Macon has a broad base of economic, cultural, historical, tourism, and corporate resources. Macon is the very heart of Georgia, both in location and culture.

We are calling upon great leaders and philanthropists with community spirit to accept the challenge and invest in Macon's future.

For more information visit our Web site at www.newtownmacon.com or call us at 912-722-9909. ❋

• Photo by Ken Krakow

GEORGIA POWER
Altec

CHAPTER FIFTEEN

15

Networks

Photo by Ken Krakow

COX COMMUNICATIONS

Information has always been a competitive advantage. In today's world, information is a necessity and information now is an advantage. Cox Communications Middle Georgia uses tomorrow's technologies to make sure that Middle Georgia families, students and businesses have the competitive advantage of nearly unlimited high-capacity high-speed access to information sources anywhere in the world!

Cox Communications Middle Georgia's parent company, Cox Communications, Inc., is the leader in bringing broadband telecommunications services to the communities it serves. From high-security telecommunications systems for military installations to broadband high-speed internet access for residential customers and businesses large and small, Cox offers the telecommunications services and support of tomorrow. Cox's redundant fiber optic and coaxial broadband technologies offer telecommunications capacity, capability, and reliability that is unmatched by other technologies and service providers.

Locally, Cox Communications Middle Georgia provides the telecommunications products and services of tomorrow to insure that the Central Georgia region remains in step with much larger major metropolitan areas in the country. This capability gives businesses the competitive advantage of information now, allowing them to take advantage of the quality of life in Middle Georgia and all the telecommunication capacity of a more populated metropolitan area.

Cox Communications Middle Georgia also remains true to its roots in offering families and businesses the very best in quality video cable television services. Cox provides analog and digital cable television services to more than 75,000 residential and business customers. Choice is the key to achieving high customer satisfaction. Cox customers can select from a basic package of 18 channels all the way up to a digital quality selection of 200 channels, with a variety of choices in between. Again, Cox uses its fiber optic and coaxial broadband network to insure that customers enjoy the highest possible quality and reliability in their cable service.

A cornerstone tenant of Cox's operating philosophy is community involvement. Cox is a partner in education and provides free cable television service and supplies free curriculum materials and teacher support to over 90 schools in its service area. Annually, Cox contributes over $1 million in charitable contributions and in-kind public service announcements and projects, not to mention the countless hours of community service donated by Cox employees.

Finally, Cox knows that the secret to its long-term success is its people. Cox supports the continued growth and development of its people with initiatives like Cox University, an award-winning internet-based educational and training resource that employees can use to tailor their own learning and development. Cox offers tuition reimbursement programs, employee stock purchase programs, 401K and pension programs among the long list of benefits available to employees. ❋

• Cox Communications Middle Georgia remains true to its roots in offering families and businesses the very best in quality telecommunications services. Cox serves more than 75,000 residential and business customers in Bibb, Houston, Jones, and Peach counties. Photo by Ken Krakow

GEORGIA POWER

Georgia Power, a unit of Southern Company, has been providing electricity to Georgia for more than a century. The company takes great pride in what it has helped the State of Georgia to accomplish and has confidence that it will continue to be a positive force in Georgia. Preston Arkwright, the company's first president, coined its motto: "A Citizen Wherever We Serve," providing a vision that has guided the way for generations of Georgia Power people.

The Georgia Power story began on December 1883, when Georgia Electric Light Company of Atlanta received a franchise to provide "electric lights for stores, dwellings, machine shops, depots... or to introduce said lights wherever desired." The company purchased its first electric light plant in 1884.

Today, Georgia Power is the largest subsidiary of Southern Company, the nation's largest generator of electricity. An investor-owned, tax-paying utility, Georgia Power serves 1.8 million retail and wholesale customers, covering 57,000 of the state's 59,000 square miles and all but six of the state's 159 counties.

Georgia Power's top priority is taking care of its customers. This means keeping reliability high and power rates low. The company's employees work with customers to help them improve efficiency in their homes, businesses, and communities. The company offers a variety of incentives and pricing options that allow Georgians to use electricity more efficiently and to control their energy costs.

Electric cars, buses, and trams offer an immediate solution to many of the world's pressing environmental pollution problems. In 1993, Georgia Power opened the Electric Vehicle Research Center to collect performance data on electric vehicles, batteries, charging stations, and other components. Georgia Power employees participate in Southern Company's corporate electric vehicle leasing program, which is currently the largest of its kind in the United States.

Through the years, Georgia Power has received numerous awards for innovations in the field of economic development. Drawing on more than 60 years' experience of matching the location needs of thousands of companies with resources of Georgia communities, the company's internationally acclaimed economic development group offers unparalleled expertise and world-class technical resources. Businesses looking to relocate or expand their companies can utilize the department's project management expertise and the Georgia Resource Center to identify the best place in Georgia to locate, saving considerable money and effort.

Georgia Power will continue to be an integral part of communities throughout the State for years to come. ❋

• (top) Georgia Power Company is helping to lead the way in bringing Alternative Fueled Vehicles such as this all-electric RAV4 to Middle Georgia.

• (left) Macon's Historic Terminal Station was saved from demolition when Georgia Power purchased it. It is now an integral piece of Downtown Revitalization plans.
Photos by William Zachary

RAGIN COMMUNICATIONS GROUP, INC. (WIRELESS WAREHOUSE)

The Ragin Communications Group, Inc.'s (Wireless Warehouse) Colonial Mall Macon kiosk store, which opened in November of 1999, was one of Middle Georgia's first Sprint PCS locations. In 2000, Wireless Warehouse, which also has two stores in Atlanta, opened three more Middle Georgia locations: in North Macon at 116 Riverside Parkway, Suite C, a DIRECTV kiosk in the Macon Mall, and one in Perry.

Wireless Warehouse, which retails Sprint PCS products, is owned by Leland K. Ragin, Jr., a Middle Georgia native who decided to open his stores in this area because he "wanted to bring digital clarity to the Middle Georgia area." Services offered by Sprint PCS, Ragin says, "include free long distance, wireless web (Internet access from your PCS phone), and free nationwide roaming on the Sprint PCS network."

Wireless Warehouse also offers Metro Call Paging, which, according to Ragin, is the number one paging company in the United States. Metro Call Paging, available with several plan options, offers local, statewide, as well as two-way paging, regional, and nationwide paging services. "You can virtually be in 86 percent of the country and receive paging," Ragin says.

Wireless Warehouse is a multifaceted communications company driven to provide wireless wholesale pricing to its retail customers. "Most of our prices are 30 to 50 percent less than our competitors, on the average," Ragin continues. He says that by providing Sprint PCS—"the clear alternative to cellular"—a consumer also has the freedom of no contracts, free long distance, and free nationwide roaming on the Sprint PCS digital network. Sprint PCS was also the first communications company to offer wireless web service on their PCS phones.

Wireless Warehouse also offers DIRECTV services to the residential and business community. DIRECTV offers more than 200 channels for less cost than the average cable rate. Direct TV, which has become the leader of satellite service providers, offers easy installation and affordable rate plans.

Wireless Warehouse is also a BellSouth Mobility, Nextel, and Powertel authorized agent and is able to provide a broader spectrum of wireless communications to the consumer. Wireless Warehouse now offers BellSouth, Nextel, and Powertel cellular phones, BellSouth and Powertel prepaid cellular service, and BellSouth.Net Internet services. Wireless Warehouse specializes in wireless accessories for all makes and models of wireless phones and pagers. The prices are offered wholesale to the consumer. Wireless Warehouse is one-stop wireless shopping provider for your home, business, or family use.

Wireless Warehouse offers all its features worldwide to consumers on its Web site. For more information contact Wireless Warehouse at www.wirelesswarehouseonline.com.

Wireless Warehouse was honored by Sprint PCS as the Southeastern Regional Retailer of the Year for 1999, "and with our growth projections for new locations statewide, it should remain the leading wireless provider for Sprint PCS far into the new millennium," concludes Ragin.

Ragin Communications, Inc., and Wireless Warehouse have made an enormous effort to get involved with the community by being members of the Mayor's Youth Advisory Council, Greater Macon Chamber of Commerce, Adopt-A-Role Model, and the One for the Kids Foundation. Mr. Ragin was also honored by being selected to the Class of 2001 Leadership Macon. By being involved in these organizations, Ragin Communications has laid the foundation for youth and economic development in Middle Georgia. ❋

• Photo by Ken Krakow

ACCESS INTEGRATED NETWORKS

Access Integrated Networks is a telecommunications company with a remarkable focus on customer care. Formed in Macon in 1996 as a direct result of the opportunities created by the passage of the Telecommunications Act of 1996, the founders of the company realized that the deregulation of the local telecommunications marketplace would revolutionize the industry and foster new, exciting options for small- and medium-size businesses.

"We incorporated with the intent of going into the local exchange telephone business," said Tom Wright, president and CEO of the company. "In September of 1997 we became certified, and we were then Macon's first competitive local telephone service. We put our first customers on our service at the time."

A vision of being a different kind of telecommunications provider emerged early on. Access's philosophy is to clearly distinguish itself in the marketplace by offering its customers cost-effective, technologically dependable products and post-sale customer care that would be unrivaled in the industry.

The benefits of Access Integrated Networks allow each customer to:

- Lower business expenses. Switching to Access for local service will save on monthly service rates for existing lines. Access will customize a telecommunications package to fit each business.
- Keep existing numbers and directory listings. Customers won't have incorrect information out there because numbers remain the same.
- Select from a full range of products and services. Customers can choose from local telephone service, long distance service, voicemail, hunting/rollover, travel cards, 800/888 service, and much more.
- Receive realistic communications solutions for their business. Access representatives will meet with each customer to discuss their needs and issues for practical communications solutions.
- Interact with Access with no contracts and only one bill. Access has a simple process for ease of service. Customers are not tied to contracts and receive one bill for all Access telecommunications services.
- Receive unmatched Focused Care. Focused Care is the branded standard of service each Access customer receives. Focused Care standards include friendly personal service and expert telecom advice with every call. Focused Care representatives are also empowered to answer customer questions in order to give each customer the most hassle-free service possible.

Now providing service to businesses in nine states throughout the Southeastern U.S., Access continues to supply innovative communications services tailored to each customer's needs. Through the company's Focused Care program and office communications solutions, Access anticipates even more growth.

"Access Integrated Networks provides an alternative to the incumbent telephone company," said Wright. "We distinguish ourselves by providing unsurpassed customer service and lower rates for local telephone service, long-distance service, and other communications-related services. Those who have previously experienced problems dealing with the incumbent find it pleasant to be able to reach and talk to a human being so quickly when they have a problem or a question."

Access Integrated Networks is referred to by Wright as "probably the most exciting thing happening in Macon today," and projects a total employment of over 500 by 2004. In its first four years of business, the company had almost 30,000 telephone lines. "As always," said Wright, "our success depends upon the competence, customer focus, and professionalism of our employees." ❋

• (top left) Access Integrated Networks Management Team. From left: Tom Wright, president and CEO; Rodney Page, vice president of Marketing & Strategic Development; Randy Smith, executive vice president of Operations; George Forbes, vice president of Information Technology; and Wayne Ellis, vice president of Human Resource Development.

• (below) Access Integrated Networks Focused Care Representative.

CHAPTER SIXTEEN

16

Real Estate, Development, & Construction

Photo by Pat McDonogh

WARREN ASSOCIATES INC.

Warren Associates Inc., commercial building contractors, will be celebrating its 30th anniversary in April 2001. The company was founded by C. Warren Selby Sr., who had a number of years' experience locally in the construction business before he started his own in 1971. Selby's son, Warren Selby Jr., who worked for his father while growing up, joined the business in the early 1980s after receiving a bachelor of science degree in building construction from Auburn University. In 1993, the founder's son bought the company from his father, who now serves as chairman of the board. The Selbys, however, have a history of three generations of being involved in the building industry; Warren Selby Sr.'s father-in-law was also a builder.

"I've actually been involved in the building business basically all my life," said Warren Selby Jr., who watched his father's business grow dramatically during the 1980s. He said the company was even recognized in 1989 by *Inc.* magazine as one of the fastest growing private companies in the South.

• (right) Peyton Anderson Health Center.
• (below) Poplar Medical Investments.

Commercial contractors, Warren Associates Inc. primarily focuses on the construction of churches, medical facilities, schools, and banks, specializing in large commercial projects, usually within a 70-mile radius of Macon.

"Over the years," said Selby, "we've established a client base of repeat customers due to the quality of workmanship we perform. One thing that sets us apart from other contractors is that people know our ability to handle complex issues, or projects." Selby explained this by saying that his company can handle jobs that involve working in places or areas that are hard to get to. "We've done a lot of historical renovation and restoration," he added. "While we were renovating the Macon Health Club to accommodate the City Club on the fourth floor, we had to keep the building in operation."

Selby said many of his company's projects have been those that were restrained by their surrounding environment. These projects, he said, have involved a number of medical facilities, including a project at the Medical Center of Central Georgia where the Emergency Room had to be open while nearby construction was underway.

Several of the more notable projects undertaken in the past by Warren Associates Inc. include the construction of Weaver Middle School on Heath Road, the Wellness Center on Northside Drive, and the Poplar Physicians' renovation at the corner of Poplar Street and MLK Jr. Boulevard in Macon, as well as Houston County Middle School, and Twiggs County High School. The company also was the contractor for the Peyton Anderson Health Education Center, a medical-education facility, at the corner of Spring and Hemlock streets, as well as a number of banks, including branches for First Liberty Bank, Rivoli Bank, and Security Bank.

Warren Associates Inc. also recently constructed the Olson Library at Stratford Academy and the third expansion at Martha Bowman Memorial United Methodist Church.

As for the future, the company has a number of projects in the making. One of these, Sports Town, will be the largest indoor sports arena in Middle Georgia. A 100,000-square-foot facility, Sports Town, which will be located off I-75 at Bass Road, is scheduled for completion in 2001.

Another future project is the approximately 70,000-square-foot Intergenerational Activities Center at the Methodist Children's Home. The center, said Selby, is a multi-use facility "that's been a dream of the Children's Home since the late 1800s."

Warren Associates Inc. not only changes the face of Macon through its projects, but also through the recognition its projects receive. In May 2000, Warren Associates Inc. was presented with an Honorable Mention in the Georgia Branch, Associated General Contractors of America, 2000 Build Georgia Award for its work on the $2.5 million renovation of Poplar Medical Investments This prestigious award is the first Build Georgia Award for Macon, Georgia. ✺

THE RAMSBOTTOM COMPANY

The Ramsbottom Company, founded in 1975 by William D. Ramsbottom Sr., is a commercial investment real estate firm specializing in all aspects of commercial and investment real estate properties such as retail and office development, site selection, build-to-suits, shopping center development, investment partnership, and commercial brokerage.

Bill Ramsbottom Sr., President of the company, received a B.S. degree from Georgia Tech and was granted the prestigious CCIM Degree from the National Institute of Realtors. After his CCIM designation, he also served as a Senior Instructor for the CCIM courses for over 20 years. In 1993, he was elected National President of the Commercial Investment Real Estate Institute and served as a member of the board of directors and the executive committee for several years. He remains today a member of the Institute's Governing Council. Ramsbottom is also a life member of the Middle Georgia Board of Realtors' Million-Dollar Club. He has been very active in the Macon community, having served as president and a member of boards of directors for various organizations.

Ramsbottom's son, William D. (Billy) Ramsbottom Jr., who is vice president of the company, joined the firm in 1988 and has also been granted the CCIM designation from the National Institute of Realtors. Like his father, he is active in the Macon community, having served on boards of various organizations. He is also a past president of the Boys and Girls Club of Central Georgia. Both men enjoy the combined business and family relationship and get rather sentimental about it. "I'm the luckiest guy in the world," Billy Ramsbottom said. "He's the best real estate guy in Macon, and I got to do exactly what I wanted to do right out of college." His father enjoys having his son work with him because it allows him to pass on the business and know that it will outlive him. "Besides," said Bill Ramsbottom Sr., "I just like being around him; it's a unique pleasure that every father should have, and not all do."

"We don't really have a very formal division of work," Bill Ramsbottom Sr. said. "I like to do certain things, and Billy gravitates to what he likes to do." Ramsbottom Sr. handles the initial stages of putting the deals together, and Ramsbottom Jr. handles the nuts and bolts of developing, building, and selling commercial properties.

The company has purchased and developed a number of properties, including shopping centers. Its tenant profile is impressive, including major merchants such as Kroger, Bruno's, K-Mart, Wal-Mart, SteinMart, Carolina Pottery, Eckerd, RadioShack, Books-A-Million, Pier One Imports, Lowe's, HEALTHSOUTH, Georgia Power, Georgia Natural Gas, and BELLSOUTH Mobility, as well as smaller tenants such as BLOCKBUSTER, Mail Boxes Etc., and others. "We also represent other owners, and we do a high volume of parcel sales to national chains in banking, gasoline, and food industries, as well as other institutions," said Ramsbottom Sr., "oftentimes as part of our shopping center developments."

The Ramsbottom Company also enjoys involvement in the industrial and warehouse aspects of the real estate industry, representing owners and tenants in the leasing of properties as well as through ownership developments. Currently underway is a warehouse development at I-475 and Thomaston Road that will meet the user needs for a number of companies as well as a 150,000-square-foot building to a national tenent PACTIV and a 60,000-square-foot building to Northrop.

The new millennium finds this progressive company involved in the property sales and development of a new Wal-Mart store in Northeast Macon, with another Wal-Mart site being contracted on Eisenhower Parkway in Macon. On the horizon are numerous shopping center sites to be developed in the expanding Warner Robins area, with the company also being involved in the development of over 3,000 acres of land, owned by various entities, in areas such as Houston Lake Road, Russell Parkway, Watson Boulevard, and the Georgia 247 Connector. "We are also working on numerous sites throughout Georgia and South Carolina for Walgreens," said Ramsbottom Jr.

Bill Ramsbottom Sr. attributes much of the success of the Macon real estate market to its central location in the state and its access to transportation via I-75, I-475, and I-16. He believes that any future transportation improvements will only enhance Macon's growth in the future. The company's main development will continue to include grocery-anchored shopping centers, industrial warehousing, build-to-suits, office development, and all the tenants and property owners associated with commercial properties. The Ramsbottom Company is located in the heart of historical downtown Macon at 892 Mulberry Street and has been described as the finest "boutique" commercial real estate company in the state of Georgia. ✵

• Father and son, William D. Ramsbottom Sr. and William D. Ramsbottom Jr. have been working side by side in Macon since 1988. Together they examine plans while overseeing construction of the HiFi Buys site. Photo by Ken Krakow

MACONPOWER

Listening to customers and providing needed services is what MaconPower does. The approach used in meeting those needs is what really separates MaconPower from its competitors. The company operates on a few simple philosophies.

First, take care of customers. Treat them with the care and respect that they deserve. Second, take care of employees by treating them according to the Golden Rule. Help them realize their potential, what they want to do and accomplish. Then, help them attain the education, knowledge, and experience that they need to reach their goals. Third, each employee must have the dedication and the desire to pass their knowledge on to the people who report to them. Fourth, after arming the employee with the necessary knowledge, experience, and company culture, MaconPower is able to turn them loose with the empowerment that they have earned and deserve to interact with fellow employees, serve customers, and solve problems. Finally, MaconPower encourages all employees through leadership giving to contribute back to the community where employees live, work, play, and raise children.

Almost any drive around Central Georgia will bring a passerby across the familiar man hurling the thunderbolt plastered on red and white vans, signs, trucks, and trailers. The MaconPower logo is the symbol of quality, dependability, commitment, and a job well done. In the electrical contracting industry, MaconPower prides itself on consistently delivering the project on time, within the budget, and to the customers' satisfaction.

As part of its commitment to providing customer and employee satisfaction, MaconPower prides itself on being one of the safest places to work in the entire construction industry. As Danny Gibson, founder and vice president would say, "no other aspect of the company receives the focus that safety does. We pride ourselves on being a fun, safe place to work. We are committed to the assurance that every employee will return home just as fit and healthy as when they went to work, and that all property which we contact will be left in as good as or better condition than when we arrived."

The company's commitment and dedication to the community is apparent through its many worthwhile endeavors such as its work with Habitat for Humanity or its annual contribution to Macon's Cherry Blossom Festival, with which MaconPower has earned the distinction of being the Official Electrical Contractor. The company always has, and always will, return a minimum of 10 percent of its after-tax earnings back to the community.

MaconPower, founded in 1990, is a division of a company that has been in existence for over 50 years. The parent company, PPC, was founded in Milwaukee, Wisconsin, in 1947, and in 1979, MetroPower, the division of which MaconPower is a part, began operations in Georgia. The entire company has enjoyed planned and consistent growth for the entirety of its existence.

With a reputation and commitment to provide world class service, and being part of a company that has been providing on-site electrical service and construction for over 50 years, existing and potential customers can be guaranteed satisfaction when they rely on MaconPower for all their electrical and related needs. ❋

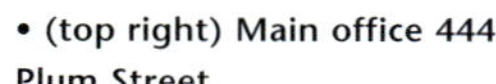

• (top right) Main office 444 Plum Street.

• (below) Ready to serve. Photos by Ken Krakow

STROUD AND COMPANY

Stroud and Company is a fullservice commercial building contractor specializing in design/build construction. Founded in 1988, and owned and operated by Charles G. Stroud, it provides a wide array of construction services. The ability to provide Butler® pre-engineered buildings, as well as conventional construction has allowed the business to completely meet its customers' needs. The company has handled the construction of approximately 140 major projects and now has over 50 employees. Its projects include many types of general contract work, including churches, offices, warehouses, and historic restoration.

In its desire to exceed customers' expectations, while at the same time developing a long-term business relationship, Stroud and Company has developed ideas it feels are vital to the successful construction of its customers' facilities. The company's extensive experience with design/build construction allows it to provide invaluable assistance in the preliminary stages of a project. By working with the architects involved, vital pre-construction issues such as budgeting and scheduling can be evaluated in a timely manner.

Each project undertaken by Stroud and Company is closely supervised by a job-site superintendent and a veteran project manager. The company's ability to develop schedules and monitor the overall performance of the project ensures the owner and the architect easy access to an informed member of the construction team.

Job-site safety, quality construction, economical performance, and timely completion are basic in providing customer satisfaction. To achieve this goal, Stroud and Company maintains a full array of qualified and dedicated field personnel. This staffing ability allows many portions of the project to be self-performed.

With an accident rate of 15 percent below the industry average, Stroud and Company's commitment to safety is apparent. An ongoing safety program is administered by an in-house safety director. OSHA trained and certified job superintendents lead weekly safety meetings. Periodic job-site reviews by outside safety consultants further assist the company in maintaining its vigil in this very important area.

Stroud and Company is a local company with a proven record of maintaining its completed facilities. The company's commitment to monitor projects after owner occupancy, together with its responsive field personnel, ensure that its many customers will always receive assistance with their post-construction needs.

Stroud and Company has a total commitment to meeting its customers' needs in an efficient manner. Its ability to provide pre-construction design/build services, competent supervision, and a capable, safety conscious workforce reflects this goal. This philosophy has allowed the company to perform a large number of negotiated contracts as well as develop a broad base of satisfied repeat customers. ❋

• (top) Historic restoration of the Blair House.

• (left) Design/build construction of Oglesby Square Shopping Center.
Photos by Ken Krakow

BURGESS CARPET ONE

Burgess Carpet One was founded as Burgess Carpet Center in 1946 by Charles D. Burgess. During his years as owner, the company increased its sales as the popularity of carpets grew as a floor covering choice. During the early years, carpets were installed and seams were hand sewn together. In the middle 1960s, Burgess developed and patented the first hot melt seaming system, which is currently used today.

In 1968, Burgess sold the patent, retired, and sold the carpet business to William E. Rivers, who is the current owner. Rivers continued to grow the business at its Orange Street location by expanding the quality of flooring and installation services. Emphasis was also put on increasing commercial sales and service.

In 1985, Rivers had a new 15,000-square-foot showroom and warehouse built at 171 Spring Street, where it is currently located. In 1990, Burgess Carpet Center became affiliated with Carpet One, a national co-op of independent floor covering dealers. When Burgess Carpet joined the co-op, there were 400 dealers and now there are more than 1,400 dealers worldwide. This affiliation allows for greater buying power and professional marketing. In 1997, Burgess changed its name to Burgess Carpet One.

Burgess' showroom has the largest selection of all types of floor covering in the Middle Georgia area. It has carpets from several leading manufacturers such as Lee's, Bigelow, Waverly, Karastan, and Evans Black. It also carries an excellent line of designer carpets and a full range of commercial carpets. Burgess Carpet One's hard surface showroom has wood flooring by Bruce and Hartco; vinyl flooring by Armstrong and Mannington; laminate flooring by Pergo, Wilsonart, and Armstrong; and ceramic tile by Shaw, Florida Tile, and Dal Tile.

Along with its extensive line of floor covering, Burgess has a large selection of machine-made and hand-made rugs, maintaining an inventory of more then 350 rugs. Its major line of machine-made rugs is from Karastan, the most recognized name in the United States. These rugs are made from 100 percent wool and are the best machine-made rugs on the market. Burgess Carpet One also maintains several lines of beautiful handmade rugs from Nourison, Pande Cameron, and Kalaty. These brands combine several types of rugs to include traditional hand-knotted rugs, soumac weave rugs, and hooked rugs. Even though these are new rugs, there are several that have an authentic antique look.

Burgess Carpet One caters to both residential and commercial customers, mainly in the Middle Georgia area, with contracts ranging from one-bedroom installations to multi-story offices, hospitals, and educational buildings. Experienced salespeople are available to assist customers with their decisions and to give estimates. Installation is provided by flooring mechanics who are CFI (Certified Flooring Installers) certified. The major focus of the business is to provide customers with quality floor coverings and installation service. The main reason Burgess Carpet One is able to give excellent service is the quality of salespeople and installers it has available and also the fact that it has a combined total of hundreds of years' experience.

In business for more than five decades, Burgess Carpet One has consistently maintained the most up-to-date selection of floor covering styles and colors. The company's success can be attributed to the mission behind its motto: "Service and Integrity Since 1946." ❋

• (top) Burgess Carpet's 15,000-square-foot showroom and warehouse built in 1985 at 171 Spring Street.

• (right) Burgess' showroom has the largest selection of all types of floor covering in the Middle Georgia area. When it comes to flooring . . . nobody does it better.

BIBLIOGRAPHY

Anderson, Nancy. *Macon: A Pictorial History.* Virginia Beach: The Donning Company, 1979.

Butler, John C. *Historical Record of Macon and Central Georgia.* Macon: J.W. Burke Company, 1879; rpt. Macon: Middle Georgia Historical Society, 1969.

Escott, Paul D. and David R. Goldfield, eds. *The South for New Southerners.* Chapel Hill: University of North Carolina Press, 1991.

Freeman, Scott. *Midnight Riders: The Story of the Allman Brothers Band.* Boston: Little, Brown and Company, 1995.

Grisamore, Ed and Bill Buckley. *Once Upon A Whoopee: A Town, A Team, A Song, A Dream.* Macon: Mercer University Press, 1998.

Jones, Bill Walker. *Vocational Legacy: Biography of Dudley Mays Hughes.* Dry Branch, 1976.

Meeks, Catherine. *Macon's Black Heritage: The Untold Story.* Macon: Tubman African American Museum, 1997.

Prater, Vickie Leach. *Macon in Vintage Postcards.* Charleston: Arcadia Publishing, 1999.

Reagan, Frank, and others. *History of Macon: The First One Hundred Years 1823-1923.* Macon: *Macon News*, 1929; rpt. Macon: *Macon Telegraph*/Williams & Canady, 1998.

Sawyer, Susan S. *A Hospital Without Walls: The First 100 Years of The Medical Center of Central Georgia, 1895-1995.* Chattanooga, TN: Parker Hood Press, Inc.

Sharifpour, Kambiz. *A Colorful Journey Through Macon.* Edited by Charles H. Snider. Macon: Panaprint, Inc., 1994.

Simms, Kristina. *Macon, Georgia's Central City: An Illustrated History.* Chatsworth: Windsor Publications, 1989.

Styons, Robert Benton. *The History of Macon College: From Its Founding through Its 25th Anniversary.* Macon: Macon College, 1993.

ACKNOWLEDGEMENTS

The writer would like to thank the following businesses and organizations for information obtained from their Web sites: Armstrong World Industries; Bibb County Public Schools; Boulevard Art Gallery; Brown & Williamson Tobacco; Bureau of Labor Statistics; U.S. Department of Labor; China Clay Producers Association; Coliseum Medical Center; Douglass Theatre; Dry Branch Kaolin Company; Flint Energies; Fort Valley State University; Georgia Children's Museum; Georgia National Fairgrounds; Georgia Power; Georgia Sports Hall of Fame; GIGA, Inc.; Lane Packing; Macon Arts Alliance; Macon Mall; Macon Northside Hospital; Macon Police Department; Macon State College; Macon Technical Institute; Macon Telegraph; Macon Water Authority; Macon Whoopee; Medical Center of Central Georgia; Mercer University; Museum of Arts & Sciences; Norfolk Southern; Ocmulgee National Monument; Population Estimates Program, Population Division, U.S. Census Bureau; Robins AFB; Saddle Creek Corporation; University of Georgia Business Outreach Services/Small Business Development Center; Wesleyan College; and YKK (U.S.A.) Inc.

All archival images appear courtesy of the Middle Georgia Archives, Washington Memorial Library, Macon, Georgia. The editor would like to thank Muriel Jackson of the Middle Georgia Archives and David Clark, who both conducted extensive photographic research.

The editor also would like to express appreciation to the following photographers for their participation in the project: Beau Cabell, Sherry DiBari, Woody Marshall, Thomas Metthe, Robert Seay, and Leah Yetter.

ENTERPRISE INDEX

IKON Office Solutions
1738 Bass Road
Building 1
Macon, Georgia 31210
Phone: 478-405-2600
Fax: 478-405-2593
E-mail: dveal@ikon.com
www.ikon.com
Pages 110-111

Macon Centreplex
200 Coliseum Drive
Macon, Georgia 31217-8098
Phone: 478-751-9152
Fax: 478-751-9154
E-mail: info@maconcentreplex.com
www.maconcentreplex.com
Pages 168-169

The Macon Orthopaedic and Hand Center
840 Pine Street, Suite 500
Macon, Georgia 31201
Phone: 478-745-4201
Fax: 478-745-0689
E-mail: mo7980@aol.com
www.maconortho-hand.com
Pages 146-147

MaconPower
444 Plum Street
Macon, Georgia 31201
Phone: 478-745-5400
Fax: 478-745-5405
E-mail: danny@metropower.com
www.maconpower.com
Page 184

Mercer University
1400 Coleman Avenue
Macon, Georgia 31207
Phone: 478-301-2700
Fax: 478-301-4124
E-mail: mercerinfo@mercer.edu
www.mercer.edu
Pages 126-129

Mount de Sales Academy
PO Box 6136
851 Orange Street
Macon, Georgia 31208
Phone: 478-751-3240
Fax: 478-751-3241
E-mail: srosina@mds.macon.ga.us
www.mds.macon.ga.us
Page 132

NewTown Macon
Terminal Station
200 Cherry Street
Macon, Georgia 31201
Phone: 478-722-9909
Fax: 478-722-9906
E-mail: newtown@redi.net
www.newtownmacon.com
Page 172

Pactiv
PO Box 10187
Macon, Georgia 31297
Phone: 478-781-1474
Fax: 478-781-9636
www.pactiv.com
Page 162

Piedmont Orthopaedic and Sports Medicine
4660 Riverside Park Boulevard
Macon, Georgia 31210
Phone: 478-474-2114
Fax: 478-474-5043
Pages 148-149

Ragin Communications Group, Inc. (Wireless Warehouse)
116 Riverside Parkway, Suite C
Macon, Georgia 31210
Phone: 478-471-PCS1 (7271)
Fax: 478-405-5949
E-mail: ragincom@aol.com
wirelesswarehouseonline.com
Page 178

The Ramsbottom Company
892 Mulberry Street
Macon, Georgia 31201
PO Box 57401
Macon, Georgia 31208
Phone: 478-743-7200
Fax: 478-743-2214
E-mail: billramsbottom@worldnet.att.net
Page 183

Secure Health Plans of Georgia
3920 Arkwright Road, Suite 405
Macon, Georgia 31210
Phone: 478-314-2400
Fax: 478-314-2437
www.shpg.com
Page 150

Stroud and Company
PO Box 2551
Macon, Georgia 31203
Phone: 478-743-5097
Fax: 478-788-0094
E-mail: cgs@stroudandcompany.com
Page 185

SunTrust Bank, Middle Georgia
606 Cherry Street
Macon, Georgia 31201
Phone: 478-741-2265
www.suntrust.com
Pages 114-115

Wachovia Corporation
484 Mulberry Street
Macon, Georgia 31213
Phone: 478-750-2021
Fax: 478-742-5110
www.wachovia.com
Page 120

Walthall Oil Company
PO Box 1203
2510 Allen Road
Macon, Geogia 31202
Phone: 478-781-1234
Fax: 478-784-0148
E-mail: fwalthall@walthall-oil.com
www.walthall-oil.com
Pages 160-161

Warren Associates Inc.
PO Box 6098
2760 Roff Avenue
Macon, Georgia 31208
Phone: 478-746-7306
Fax: 478-746-6118
Page 182

YKK Corporation of America
One Parkway Center
1850 Parkway Place, Suite 300
Marietta, Georgia 30067
Phone: 770-261-6120
Fax: 770-261-6148
www.ykkamerica.com
Pages 158-159

INDEX